INDEPENDENCE
D1503757

GREAT WORKSHOPS
FROM FINE WOODWORKING

WITHDRAWN

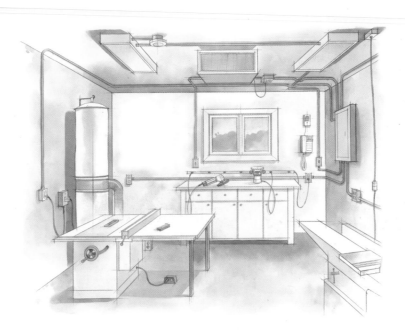

The Editors of Fine Woodworking

The Taunton Press

© 2008 by The Taunton Press, Inc.
All rights reserved.

The Taunton Press

The Taunton Press, Inc., 63 South Main Street, PO Box 5506, Newtown, CT 06470-5506
e-mail: tp@taunton.com

Editor: Nicole Palmer
Copy editor: Seth Reichgott
Indexer: Jay Kreider
Jacket/Cover design: Renato Stanisic
Layout: Laura Lind Design

Library of Congress Cataloging-in-Publication Data
Great workshops from Fine woodworking / the editors of Fine woodworking.
     p. cm.
  ISBN 978-1-56158-949-4
  1. Workshops. 2. Woodwork. I. Fine woodworking.

TT152.G73 2007
684'.08--dc22

                    2007025844

Printed in the United States of America
10 9 8 7 6 5 4 3 2 1

The following manufacturers/names appearing in *Great Workshops* are trademarks: Bessey
K Body®, Better Life Technology®, Bilco®, Costco®, Delta®, De-Sta-Co®, DRIcore®,
Ecogate®, Econ-o-watt®, Firex®, Formica®, GE®, Jet®, Leeson®, Lee Valley Tools®, Lexan®,
Lock-tile®, Oneida®, Osram®-Sylvania®, Philips®, Plexiglas®, Plugmold®, Quick-Grip®
clamps, Resilia®, Sears®/Craftsman®, SECO®, Supersaver®, Trane®, Watt-miser®, York®

Working wood is inherently dangerous. Using hand or power tools improperly or ignoring
safety practices can lead to permanent injury or even death. Don't try to perform operations
you learn about here (or elsewhere) unless you're certain they are safe for you. If something
about an operation doesn't feel right, don't do it. Look for another way. We want you to enjoy
the craft, so please keep safety foremost in your mind whenever you're in the shop.

Acknowledgments

Special thanks to the authors, editors, art directors, copy editors, and other staff members of *Fine Woodworking* who contributed to the development of the articles in this book.

Contents

3 4633 00210 4006

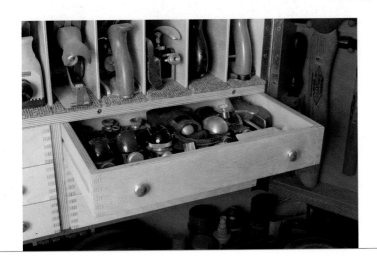

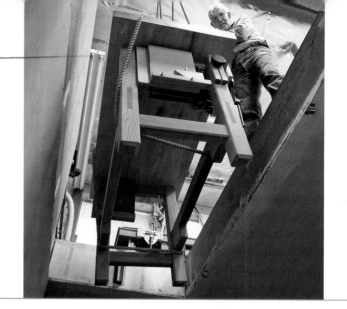

Introduction

Fine Woodworking's editors hit the road for months every year, visiting scores of real-world shops to capture projects and processes as they really happen. We see everything from clean, well-lighted places to dusty, cramped caves, where it is a wonder anything gets built. Only the best shop ideas make it into the magazine. This compilation, then, represents the best of the best, the last word on buildings, floor plans, wiring, heating, dust collection, lumber and tool storage, ergonomics, and much more. Take it from us—this is the stuff that works.

Like many people, my first shop was a basement. It was underpowered and underlit, and I addressed those issues with the help of an electrician. It was also undersized, so I built storage into every available space, and raised machines and other work surfaces to the same height for better flow. The truth is you can't always choose your shop space, but you can choose how to use it. This book offers dozens of ways to make any floor plan work better. If you are happy with your space but need an upgrade in lighting, power, or dust collection, consult this book before spending serious cash. And if you are finally ready to build your dream shop, we've got that covered, too, with floor-to-rafters profiles of the best shops we've seen.

As Joe Tracy explains on p. 8, the shop is the most important woodworking tool. Imagine a workspace where lumber is easy to handle, the air is clean, the temperature is right, every tool is close at hand, and work flows smoothly from station to station and out the door before you know it. Read on to make that happen.

—Asa Christiana,
Editor, *Fine Woodworking*

A SHOP WITH ELBOW ROOM. Much of the appeal of the shop can be traced to the more than 800 sq. ft. of floor space, plus lots of natural light and ventilation.

A Shop on Top

BY PAUL H. BRESKIN

For a good many years, I was able to get by with my three-car garage doubling as a workshop. And while all the shuffling of cars and woodworking machines made that shop far from a perfect arrangement, it provided enough space to satisfy most of my woodworking needs.

Eventually, though, as I spent more time in the less-than-ideal confines of a garage, I began to recognize the many advantages of a stand-alone shop. But there was a problem: I didn't have room on the property to expand outward. That's when I realized my dedicated shop could be had by adding a second story to the garage. Although some might consider the solution unorthodox, it provided me with an additional 800 sq. ft. of open space to devote entirely to my shop.

Like any major building project, this one came with an assortment of challenges. For starters, the foundation needed major modifications to meet building-code requirements related to the added weight of a second story. Also, because the second floor had to support a 16-in. jointer that weighs more than 1,800 lb., the floor joists had to be 2x14 lumber placed 12 in. on center, instead of the more common requirement of 2x12 lumber placed 24 in. on center. I also had to use 1¼-in.-thick tongue-and-groove plywood for the floor, instead of the normal ¾-in.-thick plywood.

Support posts always seem to get in the way in a woodworking shop. To avoid having any, I substituted an 8-in. by 16-in. steel I-beam for the typical wood ridge beam. The I-beam also served as a place to mount a chain hoist with a trolley. The trolley lets me run the hoist along nearly the full length of the shop.

To help contain shop noise, I insulated the floor, ceiling, and walls. Now, as long as the windows are closed, I can work in the shop any time of the day or night without bothering my neighbors.

Compressors are noisy, and mine is no exception. To give my ears some relief, I installed the compressor below the shop, in the garage. I use the same area for lumber storage.

The exterior of the shop, including the windows, was designed to complement the look of the house. A lot of natural light bathes the shop, thanks to a generous number of windows, plus a sliding glass door and three skylights. To help minimize noise, all of the windows, doors, and skylights are double-paned.

Thanks to all of the glass, I rarely need to have lights turned on during the day.

Keep in mind, though, that windows have one drawback: They reduce wall space. And walls are great places to hang tools or mount storage cabinets. In my shop, the walls are constructed of pine boards installed horizontally. Not only does the pine give the shop an appropriate look, but it's also a surface that readily accepts screws, nails, and pegs to hang tools.

A 6-ft. by 8-ft. bathroom, complete with a toilet, sink, and shower, occupies the northwest corner of the shop. The shower lets me clean up quickly at the end of the day before heading back to the house. The sink is more than just a place to wash my hands; it's also a brush-cleaning station and an area to sharpen edge tools with my waterstones.

My Southern California location means I don't have to worry about heating the shop, but I do have to keep it cool. Toward that end, I mounted a 16-in. by 16-in. squirrel-cage fan high on the east wall to exhaust warm air to the outside. However, because the fan pushes such a large volume of air when it runs, I need to keep one of the windows open a crack; otherwise, the airflow would be reduced considerably. Thanks to a built-in thermostat, the fan goes on and off as needed to keep the temperature under control.

At the end of the day, for safety's sake, I want to be able to shut off power to all of the electrical outlets with one switch. A separate subpanel makes that possible.

I've been in my upstairs shop for a few years now. Any doubts I might have had about the sense of building up have long since disappeared. The shop is bright, spacious, and comfortable. And the distant views of Malibu and Catalina Island I gained from my second-story vantage point aren't hard to take, either.

PAUL H. BRESKIN, an amateur woodworker for 50 years, has studied with such notable furniture makers as Ian Kirby, James Krenov, Sam Maloof, and John Nyquist. He lives in Southern California.

A Second Story Shop

In need of room for a shop but lacking space on his property to build one, Breskin looked up rather than out. His single-story, three-bay garage (see the top photo below) was expanded skyward (see the bottom photo below), producing space for an 800-sq.-ft. shop that blends comfortably with the design of his home.

Cars and Shop Coexist

By pushing the roof skyward, Breskin created a second-story space for his woodworking shop. That means family cars no longer have to compete with shop machinery for garage space.

Anything heavy or awkward is raised from the first floor, through a 4-ft. by 8-ft. trap-door, with a chain hoist and trolley that runs the full length of the I-beam.

Heavy I-beam at the ridge eliminated the need for support columns, creating an open floor pan.

Sliding glass doors

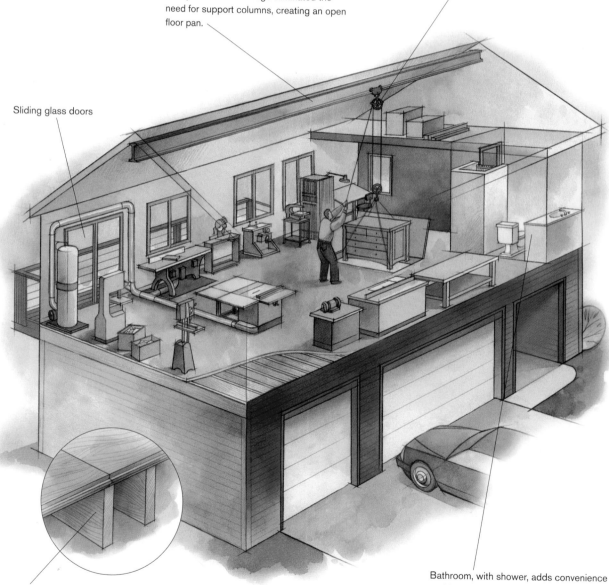

To help carry extraheavy loads from shop equipment, Breskin used 2X14 floor joists and 1¼-in.-thick tongue-and-groove plywood flooring.

Bathroom, with shower, adds convenience and helps reduce the amount of dust that gets tracked into the house.

Accessing a Second-Story Shop

Gravity is not your friend in a second-floor shop, as the biggest challenge is getting tools and materials topside. But thanks to some clever planning, Breskin has two good ways to get heavy stuff upstairs.

DRIVE-THROUGH DELIVERY

A door in the back of the garage allows Breskin to unload material close to the stairs that lead to the second-story shop. Small projects and most run-of-the-mill materials can be carried up or down the stairs with little difficulty.

A DOOR IN THE FLOOR

When heavy or awkward items can't be moved easily up or down the outside stairs, a trapdoor in the shop floor provides the best way in or out. The trapdoor is located directly under the I-beam, and with the aid of the hoist, all sorts of heavy items can be hauled up or down through the opening.

The Shop as Tool

BY JOE TRACY

1. Finishing Room

I hung an interior wall on four heavy-duty door hinges. The wall closes, making space for assembly, storage, or anything else. But when it's open, it forms an efficient little spray booth. An exhaust fan keeps finish odors away from other areas of the shop.

2. Vacuum Press

On one side of the finishing room's movable wall is my vacuum veneer press table, a hinged table on a hinged wall. When the table is needed, it drops down, but most of the time, it folds against the wall and out of the way.

3. Lumber Storage

The driveway runs up to the lumber storage area, which comes in handy when unloading wood.

4. Garage Door

Inside, I store long boards vertically, so I can get to them without unstacking a pile. I modified a garage door so it opens almost straight up—this leaves high wall space for storing boards.

5. Flooring

Stenciling and spray painting the high-density particleboard floor into 1-sq.-ft. modules makes easy work of judging lumber length.

6. Showroom
Because of its many windows and location at the shop's south end, the showroom gets plenty of natural light.

7. Sliding Barn Door
I mounted a glass door on a barn-door track. It rolls out of the way to make room for large loads going into or coming out of the shop.

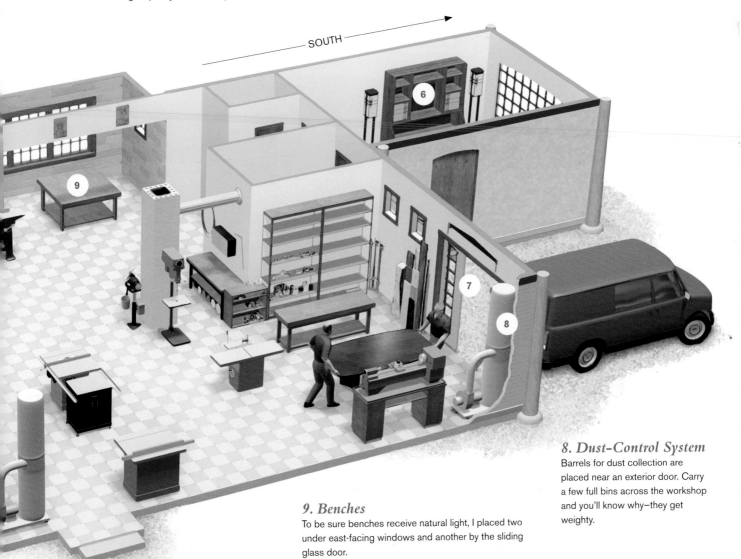

8. Dust-Control System
Barrels for dust collection are placed near an exterior door. Carry a few full bins across the workshop and you'll know why—they get weighty.

9. Benches
To be sure benches receive natural light, I placed two under east-facing windows and another by the sliding glass door.

A well-designed, well-built shop can do more for your woodworking than any new tablesaw or handplane. A good shop is a place you want to be, a safe, comfortable, well-lit space where work flows efficiently from machine to bench to finishing area. Of course, building a shop is a good deal more expensive proposition than buying a new

tablesaw. Whatever your situation—even if you just want to retrofit a basement or garage—you won't go wrong if you think of your shop as a complex functioning tool that calls for continual sharpening and adjustment.

The first step in creating a new workshop is determining a floor plan that will make it an efficient and enjoyable

place to work. You don't want your tools simply lining the walls of the shop. Instead, consider not only the area that the tool will take up, but also what I call a tool's shadow—the amount of space around the tool that will make it accessible for ripping and crosscutting. Because my two tablesaws see more work than any of my other machines, I wanted them in central locations, but within proximity to the lumber room. I also wanted them in relatively permanent locations, but in places where I could reposition them to accommodate large or awkward boards.

No matter how big a shop is, sooner or later, materials and projects will have it straining at its seams. Flexible use of space is very important to me. Unless something is being used, I want it out of the way. The best solution to a problem is often just at the edge of our conceptual reach—disarmingly simple sometimes, but requiring a creative leap. The drawings and photos show just a few of the ways I've managed to capitalize on shop space.

When I set out to build my shop six years ago, I had a number of ideas I wanted to incorporate into the structure. I decided early on to use metal agricultural roofing, a relatively inexpensive roofing material that's extremely durable and sheds snow well, which is not an insignificant consideration here in Maine.

I framed the roof to provide deep eaves to keep as much snow, rain, and sun away from the sides and base of the building as possible. Not only does this help protect siding, all but eliminating the need for maintenance, but also it provides storage space beneath the eaves, next to the walls of the shop.

Almost all of my windows are shop-built. When I made them, I sized them to fit precisely between the wall studs for easy installation. I also placed the windows high up on the wall, near the eaves, so I have plenty of wall space inside for shelving and

DOOR STAYS OUT OF THE WAY. The author modified a regular garage door; otherwise, it would have made moving and sorting boards in the vertical storage area difficult. He hacksawed a kerf in the tracks the door rides in, then straightened them and oriented them almost vertically. Counterweighting the door makes it easy to open.

A DISAPPEARING ROUTER TABLE. Built for convenience, the author's router table can be clamped in a bench vise and ready to use in seconds. It stores out of the way just as quickly.

◄ SAVING A TOOL. The author's bandsaw was bought from an old warehouse for $40 and then reworked. The author made a plywood case for the bottom and used old sash weights to counterweight the guide post, making it easier to adjust.

▶MISTER KEEPS TOOLS COOL. Powered by compressed air, this mister blasts coolant from the reservoir onto the grinder pedestal and leading edge of the tool being ground, preventing the tool from being burned.

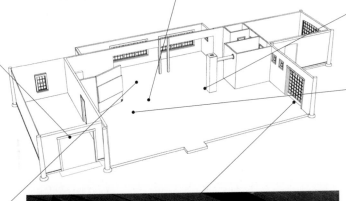

A DOOR TO EASE THE LOAD. A large door on a barn-door track slides open to make awkward loads more manageable. The author opted for a glass door to keep the shop well-lit.

SMALL TOUCHES ADD COMFORT TO A SHOP. With the author's vacuum press folded away in the movable wall, you see that a quick paint job on a simple particleboard floor breaks up the monotony of a shop. Beneath the particleboard are 2x4 sleepers and radiant-heat tubing that comes out at his feet, where it does the most good.

hanging tools—not to mention that the natural light they provide is a welcome boon to any shop.

Once inside the shop, milling of stock takes place in one section of the shop, bench work elsewhere, sanding and finishing in still other locations. Dust can be a nuisance, as well as a health hazard, and handling it is a chore. I placed all my sanding machines—a stroke sander, disc sander, inflatable drum sander, and reciprocating spindle sander—in one corner, and use a simple exhaust fan to keep dust away from other machines. I also outfitted all my major machines—the shaper, jointer, planer, and my two tablesaws—with ducts for dust collection. The stroke sander has its own collection system, and all the dust barrels are kept near doorways so they're easy to carry out and dump.

Once you get a rough idea of how you want your shop to look and function, the lay of the land begins to fill in some of the details. I sell my furniture from my shop, so the southeast corner—with its abundance of sunlight and attractive position as you approach the building—was the obvious choice for the showroom.

The location of the lumber room seemed just as logical. It's in the rear of the shop where it's easily accessible from the driveway. Boards move smoothly—on good days—from one end of the shop to the other. Overall, it's a great shop, but there's always room to improve. My next one will be even better.

JOE TRACY works wood on Mount Desert Island, Maine. With nearly 30 years of woodworking experience, he has built everything from production furniture to timber-frame houses.

THE INTENTIONAL SHOP. The author's second shop incorporates all he learned from his first effort. A scale model (see pp. 8–9) helped him work out proportions and details.

Great Shop in a Two-Car Garage

BY CURTIS ERPELDING

A workshop ought to be perfectly practical—just a place to work wood and to keep tools and materials dry and warm—but it never is. That's because it is also very personal. The problems you solve as you outfit your shop may be practical ones, but they arise for personal reasons: You make jigsaw puzzles as well as highboys; your shop is unheated in the winter and floods in the spring; you like to stand while drawing and sit down while cutting dovetails; you store your kayak for

half the year suspended from the ceiling above your milling machines.

I've had six shops over the last 20 years, and I've found that improving a shop is a matter of learning about myself and the way I work, both in general and in each specific space.

In my first shop, which was the cleared-out end of a book-storage warehouse, I hung the few tools I had accumulated on the wall a good 10 paces away from my worktable. It soon became apparent that

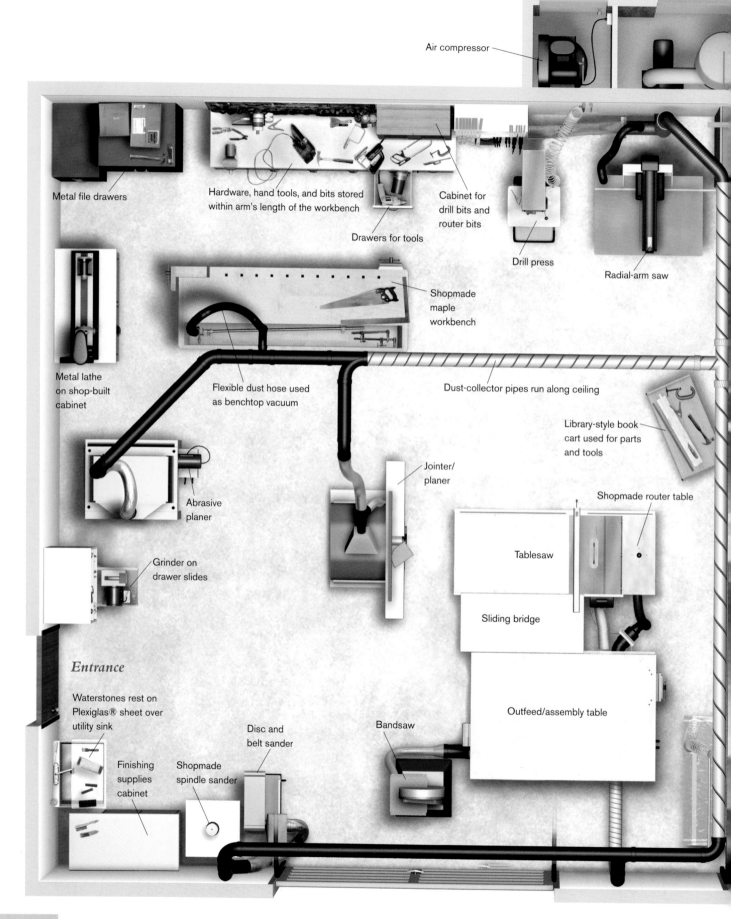

Air compressor

Metal file drawers

Hardware, hand tools, and bits stored within arm's length of the workbench

Drawers for tools

Cabinet for drill bits and router bits

Drill press

Radial-arm saw

Shopmade maple workbench

Metal lathe on shop-built cabinet

Flexible dust hose used as benchtop vacuum

Dust-collector pipes run along ceiling

Library-style book cart used for parts and tools

Abrasive planer

Jointer/ planer

Shopmade router table

Grinder on drawer slides

Tablesaw

Sliding bridge

Entrance

Outfeed/assembly table

Waterstones rest on Plexiglas® sheet over utility sink

Disc and belt sander

Bandsaw

Finishing supplies cabinet

Shopmade spindle sander

Dust collector

Open metal shelving

Cafeteria
tray trolley

Heater

Vertical
plywood
storage

Shaper

Vacuum pump
in portable box

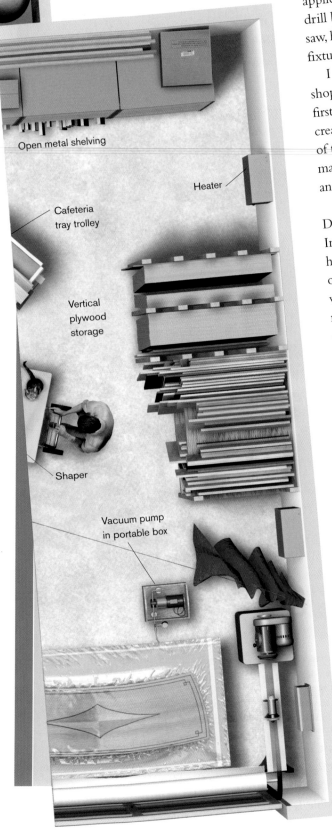

constant trips between the wall and the worktable were doing nothing for my productivity. I learned a specific lesson and applied it in my succeeding shops: Store drill bits by the drill press, sawblades by the saw, hand tools by the workbench, jigs and fixtures by the machines they were built for.

I also learned a more general rule of shop design: You'll rarely get it right the first time. It takes time and experience to create a well-functioning, efficient shop. All of the aspects of shop order—from tool and machine layout to work-flow procedures and storage solutions—evolve over time.

My grinding setup is an example of Darwinism as it applies in the workshop. In that first shop, my grinding device was a hand-operated wheel clamped to the edge of the table. It had all the disadvantages: It was slow, it took muscle, its minimal tool rest made it difficult to obtain a consistent edge, and, being clamped to the worktable, it was in the way. It didn't take too long to realize that if I was serious about making a living while using hand tools, I would have to find a better system.

The first improvement was to motorize. I salvaged an old washing-machine motor that ran at a convenient 1,725 rpm and fitted it with a white vitrified wheel. Then I went about finding a better approach to the tool-rest problem. One drawback of most tool rests is that they don't fully support the blade being sharpened. Another problem is that they force you to hold the tool or blade at an unnatural angle. I built a tool rest in the shape of an open-sided box around the grinding wheel. The wheel emerges through a slot in the top of the box the way a tablesaw blade emerges through the throat plate. This enables me to grind tools while they are lying flat and fully supported on the top of the box (see the left photo on p. 20). Even spokeshave irons and small marking knives can be precisely ground without the need for positioning fixtures. With the motor

LUMBER AND A PLACE TO CUT IT. A system of cantilevered arms provides easy-access lumber storage as well as support for a chopsaw table designed for rough-cutting planks.

small shop is imperative, and wheels help tremendously with this. I have all of my major standing machines on wheels except for my tablesaw and jointer.

The jointer and planer are near the tablesaw, which makes sense from the perspective of workflow, and it also helps with dust collection. Arranged this way, these three primary generators of dust can share the two hoses that I have hooked up to my dust collector. In my old shop, I had ceiling-mounted PVC pipe running to every machine. I found it to be overkill, and it produced enough static electricity to keep my hair standing on end much of the time. These days I simply have flexible hose running on the floor. It may be a slight nuisance to step over, but it works fine, is a more adaptable system, and doesn't mess with my hair.

The tablesaw took precedence not only in laying out the machine area but also in my tool budget. My theory of machine purchases is this: For machines I use most heavily and rely on most for precision work—tablesaw, jointer, planer, mortiser, pin-router—I cough up the money for high-quality, heavy-duty equipment. For more peripheral machines, where accuracy is less critical—edge sander, grinder, dust collector—I tend toward Taiwanese knock-offs.

Bench Area

The two main work surfaces in my bench area summarize the work I do there. One is a traditional cabinetmaker's bench, and the other is a broad assembly table. Having the two in proximity—they are parallel and stand about 6 ft. apart—is extremely functional. Both are movable (with some effort), and I can change their locations depending on what I am building.

Whereas the cabinetmaker's bench is open underneath, the assembly table is packed solid: I utilized the large space beneath the top by filling it with cabinets and heavy-duty drawers. These hold all of my handheld power tools and their accessories and much hardware. This way, the tools are stored within arm's length of where they are used. The drawers are also easily reached from the workbench. The assembly table has several outlets built in under the top, and I added one to the workbench as well.

The cabinetmaker's bench is fairly traditional, but I did make a few departures. One was to leave out a tool trough in favor of a larger work surface. I built in a tail vise, which is invaluable, but in place of a traditional shoulder vise I opted for a commercial metal side vise. I find a shoulder vise to be a bit of an impediment, and these metal vises are hard to beat with their convenient quick release, great holding power, and easy installation.

Building my own bench meant I could design it for just the way I work. Working with handplanes a lot, as I do, a good, solid bench is almost as important as a sharp blade. You want all of your energy transferred into the workpiece and the cutting action—not into a rickety bench that racks and wobbles with every stroke.

For tools used primarily at the workbench, I built shallow, two-door cabinets and hung them on the wall by the bench. They store chisels, handplanes, scrapers, spokeshaves, and other supplies. Storing tools and supplies behind doors helps with dust problems, and keeping the cabinets shallow makes for simpler storage and easier retrieval of the tools.

My approach in building storage cabinets is a little different from some. Instead of building shop furniture quickly and cheaply, I put real effort into building it. If I can save some labor or money, I do—two of the tool cabinets were extras from custom kitchens I built. But considering how much time I spend in my shop, it makes sense to please myself with the environment there. And the effort is not lost on clients who visit my shop. The cabinets demonstrate the type of

THE IMPORTANCE OF AESTHETICS. In building his storage cabinets, shop furniture, and cabinetmaker's bench, the author took the time to make things that would be visually pleasing as well as functional.

A PLACE FOR EVERYTHING. Space above the rafters is used for storing—and even drying—lumber.

good ideas I see are abundant. While visiting Tony O'Malley, a woodworker in Emmaus, Penn., I was struck by the efficiency and cleverness of his storage space. He had built storage units all around the top of his shop wall similar to the MDF units I had installed above my bandsaw, jointer, and chopsaw station.

I built them using an ultralight MDF rather than the weightier MDF of my outfeed table—the weight helps in that situation, but it isn't necessary on the wall. The light stuff is also much more pleasant to use. As O'Malley did on his shelves, I ran dadoes in the top and bottom to make the storage units adjustable and adaptable: By rearranging the ¼-in.-thick dividers, I can design separate cubbyholes for each tool.

Above both the chopsaw station and jointer, I screwed simple plywood shelves to the wall. The shelves hold screws, router bits, and drill bits and help keep everything organized. Staying organized is key to working in any shop—I hate floundering around a sloppy space trying to locate a bit or a tool. And for space reasons, organization is even more important in a small shop. I used watchmaker's cases from Lee Valley Tools® to hold screws and other hardware (see the top right photo on p. 34). With just a glance, I can find what I'm looking for.

Where MDF Falls Short

I was bent on using quick methods and economical materials, but when it came to my workbench, it was hard to accept compromise. I recently inherited an old workbench top from a friend, who had inherited it from another friend, who'd been given the bench by a boatbuilding pal many years ago. It is exactly the kind of workbench that makes you want to be a woodworker—an end vise, a front vise, a tail vise, and a heavy maple top scarred with history.

A Sho

Store ma
used to
machines, su
maximize floo

A storage shelf
and desk doesn't
height in a critica
provide storage f
other lesser-used

The machine
room of the shop
has double sliding
barn doors near the
wood-storage areas.
Weather stripping helps
keep out drafts.

A light gray
reflects lig
shells were
and make fo

**MAKING IT WORK. A well-
planned space—even if it's
small—allows plenty of room
for building furniture. Here,
Teague works on a set of cherry
dining chairs.**

I built a maple base for it and installed the same drawer boxes I'd used on an earlier bench. I don't think I could sleep at night if I stored my favorite chisels and planes in an MDF box above the bench. Instead, I made a simple cherry wall unit with two box doors. I picked my favorite and most necessary hand tools and outfitted the box with custom tool holders. It was quick work, but the unit serves all of my needs.

Though the garage required a fair amount of renovation, the shop came together quickly and works better than I ever would have imagined. A good workshop should be simple and sensible but designed with an eye toward efficiency. A sensible shop makes you work better and smarter. The best part is that when I move, the shop can be disassembled to move with me.

MATTHEW TEAGUE is a furniture maker and writer based in Nashville, Tennessee.

A
Or

BY ROS

LAY OUT THE SHOP ON GRAPH PAP
machine and workbench footprints
pieces of paper and move them aro
different configurations.

Get the Most Out of the Available Space

Through his years of experience working in a number of different shops, Day grew accustomed to having separate rooms for machine and benchwork. The partial wall in his shop separates the machine room from the bench room without closing it off entirely and making the modestly sized building feel cramped. That wall also adds significantly to the efficiency of the shop, providing plenty of storage space. Because floor space is always precious, Day went so far as to mount the compressor up high, out of the way, so that the area below could be freed up for a sharpening station.

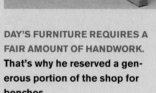

DAY'S FURNITURE REQUIRES A FAIR AMOUNT OF HANDWORK. That's why he reserved a generous portion of the shop for benches.

THE BANDSAW MAY BE PLACED CLOSE TO A WALL. Leave plenty of room fore and aft to handle long stock.

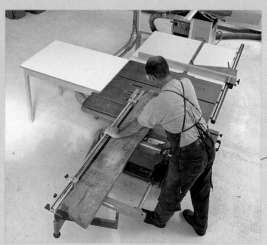

A SLIDING TABLESAW NEGATES THE NEED FOR A CHOPSAW STATION. Sheet goods and solid stock may be crosscut or ripped accurately on a sliding tablesaw.

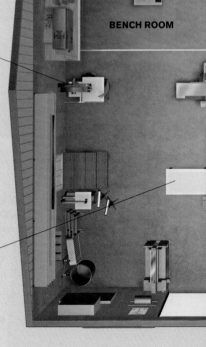

BENCH ROOM

A SIMPLE PIPE RACK FOR LUMBER. Holes drilled into the studs behind the plywood walls anchor the 2-in.-dia. galvanized pipe.

THE AIR COMPRESSOR RESTS ON AN INDUSTRIAL-STRENGTH SHELF ALONG ONE WALL. Below, the floor space is utilized for a more practical application, in this case a sharpening station.

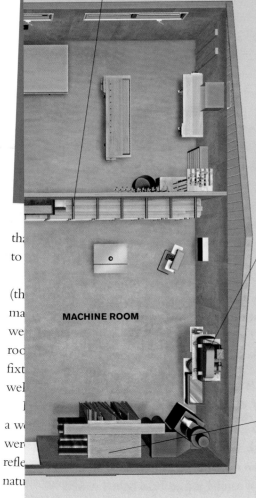

MACHINE ROOM

tha
to

(th
ma
we
roo
fixt
wel

a we
wer
refle
natu

KEEP STOCK AND ACCESSORIES NEAR APPROPRIATE MACHINERY. A wall two steps away from the tablesaw holds blades and other accessories. Plywood is also stored near the saw.

Use Computer Modeling for Paper-Free Planning in 3-D

You have a few options for planning your shop space: The first is simply to photocopy the two-dimensional models provided on p. 49 and use them to create a scale layout of your shop floor. You also can go to my website (www.yda-online.com/shopmodels.htm) and download two-dimensional images of each tool to be used either on paper or on the computer. As a third alternative, you can download the same modeling program I used and create three-dimensional plans.

The program is called SketchUp Pro (a demo version is available at www.sketchup.com, which allows 8 hours of free use). The program is easy to learn and use, even for a computer novice. If you download and learn SketchUp, feel free to go to my website and download my 3-D models for your own use, or use SketchUp to create your own.

By the way, I have used SketchUp to design every piece of furniture and cabinetry I've built over the last few years, even working out joinery details and making color choices on the computer. And I know of many other woodworkers across the country who have discovered SketchUp and put it to good use.

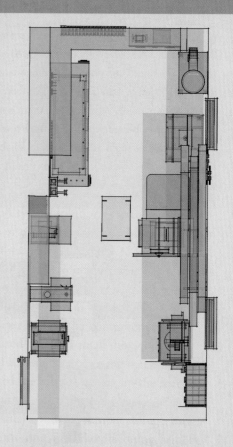

GO THREE-DIMENSIONAL FOR THE ULTIMATE PLAN. Creating his own three-dimensional CAD models allowed Yurko to plan vertical space as well as floor space, helping him locate spots for essential lumber, accessories, shelves, and cabinets.

EVERYTHING WITHIN ARM'S REACH. **Using two- and three-dimensional CAD models, Yurko crafted a bench area that packs in hand tools, air tools (and a compressor), a sharpening station, and hardware storage.**

with workpiece support on both sides—and it also accepts a minilathe. I even planned a location for all of the tools, blades, and jigs used with the tablesaw: on the operator side, for easy access.

Along the opposite long wall are the planer, combination sander, drill press, bandsaw, workbench, and compressor. Each tool has dust-collection hookups and storage space to keep the relevant tools, bits, blades, and fixtures nearby. The planer is the only tool I have to roll out into the middle of the room to use, which takes about a minute, including connecting the dust-collection hose.

Using the three-dimensional models, I also realized that even though the bandsaw's table must be higher than the adjacent workbench, I can support large pieces with a shopmade roller support clamped in the bench's front vise.

Pros and Cons of a Small Shop

For all of my planning, I must admit there simply was no room in my shop for some tools. I struggled to find a place for my wide jointer and eventually decided against shoehorning it in, instead making a fixture for my router table that joints edges quite well. My scrollsaw, the bulk of my wood supply, and some storage cabinets didn't make the cut either. These remain in a nearby room.

In many ways it's more enjoyable to work in a small space. Because most everything is only a couple of steps away, I'm much less fatigued after an evening of woodworking. The hours I spent planning have already saved me many hours of precious shop time.

JOHN YURKO is an architect and hobbyist woodworker in Asheville, North Carolina.

A Shop Built around an Island

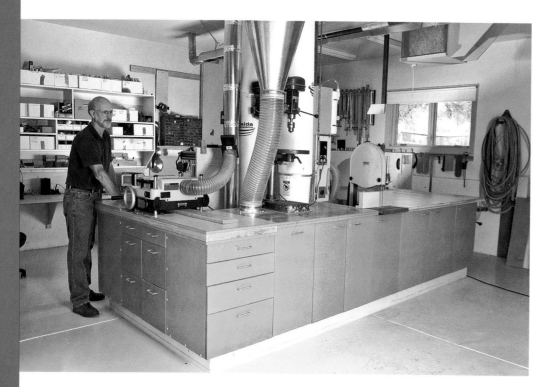

Radial-arm saw
There is 14 ft. of clearance to the left of the saw and 6 ft. to the right, allowing long boards to be crosscut with ease.

13-in. planer
The cabinets provide infeed and outfeed support, and there is clearance for boards up to 11 ft. long.

BY ALAN DeVILBISS

I'm sure every woodworker dreams of designing and building the perfect workshop. I finally got my chance after I retired as a circuit-design engineer for Hewlett-Packard. After two previous shops in two-car garages laid out conventionally with some tools around the walls and others on mobile bases, the engineer in me said there had to be a more efficient way to use space.

My design has a central grouping of stationary machines. By sharing infeed and outfeed space, I achieve maximum capacity for handling large boards in minimum floor space. An added bonus is that this design requires perhaps one-fifth of the dust-collection ductwork of a conventional shop with tools around the walls. This not only saved money but is more efficient.

Cabinets Provide Storage, Infeed/Outfeed Support

The building is 24 ft. by 40 ft., giving about 875 sq. ft. of floor space, with a 10-ft.-high ceiling. Although about half the area could be used for parking, I park only one vehicle there.

After drawing detailed plans, I marked the outline of the island base on the concrete

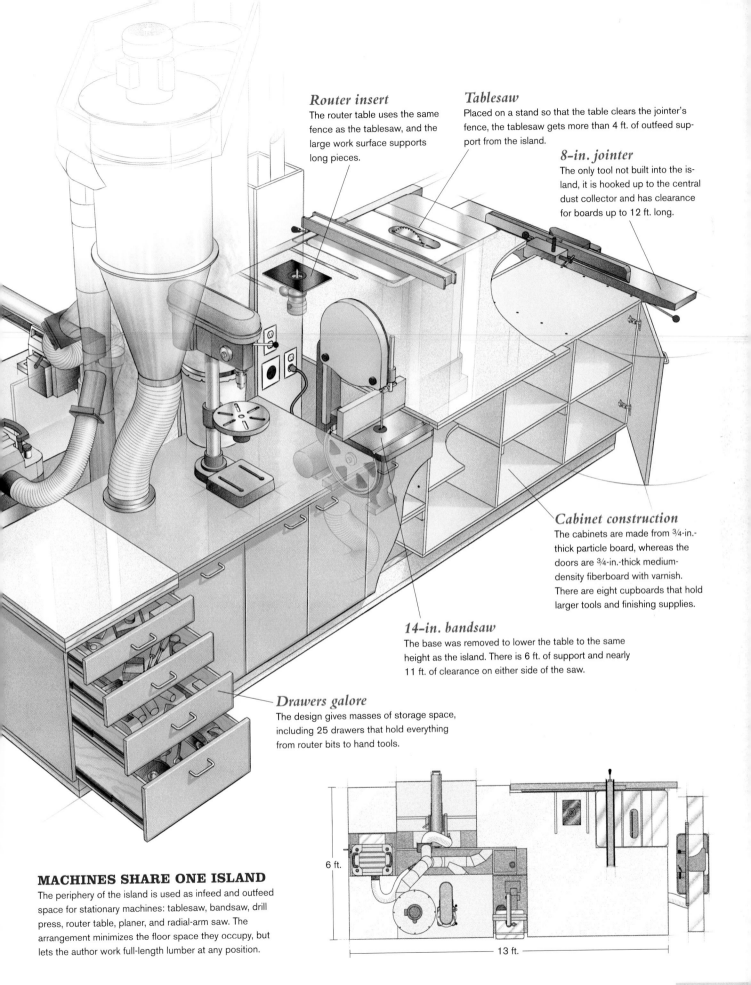

Router insert
The router table uses the same fence as the tablesaw, and the large work surface supports long pieces.

Tablesaw
Placed on a stand so that the table clears the jointer's fence, the tablesaw gets more than 4 ft. of outfeed support from the island.

8-in. jointer
The only tool not built into the island, it is hooked up to the central dust collector and has clearance for boards up to 12 ft. long.

Cabinet construction
The cabinets are made from 3/4-in.-thick particle board, whereas the doors are 3/4-in.-thick medium-density fiberboard with varnish. There are eight cupboards that hold larger tools and finishing supplies.

14-in. bandsaw
The base was removed to lower the table to the same height as the island. There is 6 ft. of support and nearly 11 ft. of clearance on either side of the saw.

Drawers galore
The design gives masses of storage space, including 25 drawers that hold everything from router bits to hand tools.

MACHINES SHARE ONE ISLAND
The periphery of the island is used as infeed and outfeed space for stationary machines: tablesaw, bandsaw, drill press, router table, planer, and radial-arm saw. The arrangement minimizes the floor space they occupy, but lets the author work full-length lumber at any position.

6 ft.

13 ft.

Work Island Allows for Efficient Dust Collection

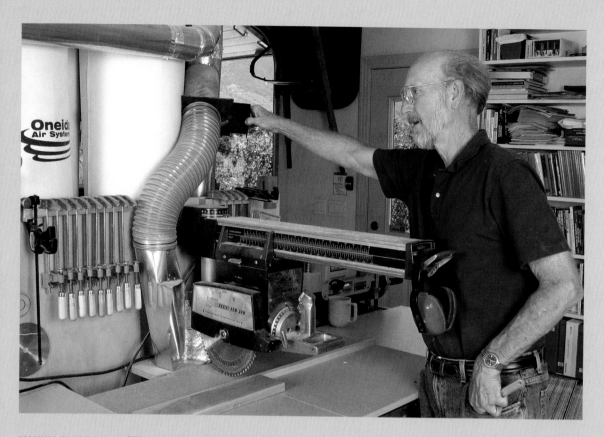

MANUAL BLAST GATES. Although the dust-collection system comes on automatically when any of the large machines are started, the blast gates are operated manually.

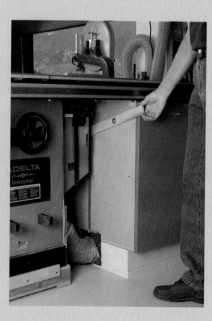

EASIER TO OPERATE. To avoid bending down, the author attached a simple lever to the blast gate for the tablesaw.

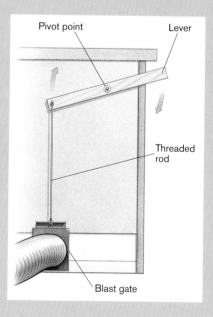

Pivot point

Lever

Threaded rod

Blast gate

CENTRALIZED DUST COLLECTION

Grouping all the machines around the island with the dust-collection system in the middle makes for short ductwork with no pipes snaking across the floor or up to the ceiling and back down again.

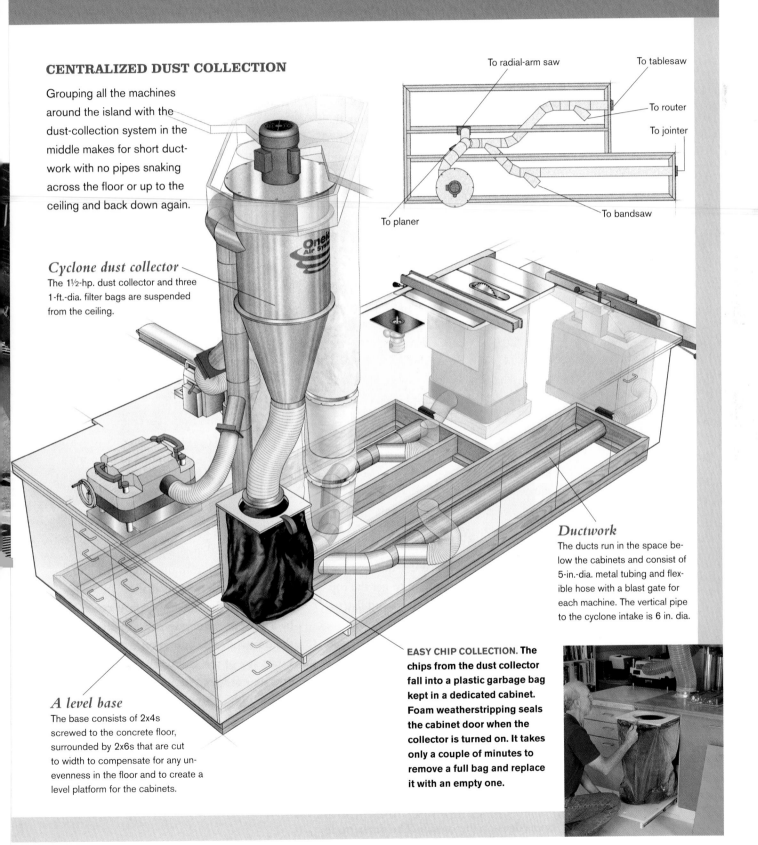

To radial-arm saw

To tablesaw

To router

To jointer

To bandsaw

To planer

Cyclone dust collector
The 1½-hp. dust collector and three 1-ft.-dia. filter bags are suspended from the ceiling.

Ductwork
The ducts run in the space below the cabinets and consist of 5-in.-dia. metal tubing and flexible hose with a blast gate for each machine. The vertical pipe to the cyclone intake is 6 in. dia.

EASY CHIP COLLECTION. The chips from the dust collector fall into a plastic garbage bag kept in a dedicated cabinet. Foam weatherstripping seals the cabinet door when the collector is turned on. It takes only a couple of minutes to remove a full bag and replace it with an empty one.

A level base
The base consists of 2x4s screwed to the concrete floor, surrounded by 2x6s that are cut to width to compensate for any unevenness in the floor and to create a level platform for the cabinets.

GOOD PLANNING ENSURES THE BEST USE OF LIMITED SPACE

To conform to zoning regulations, the footprint of McCaskill's shop couldn't exceed 40 percent of the backyard area. The building couldn't be any closer than 6 ft. to another structure or 5 ft. to the property line, and its height could not exceed 15 ft. In addition, the building's exterior had to match that of the house.

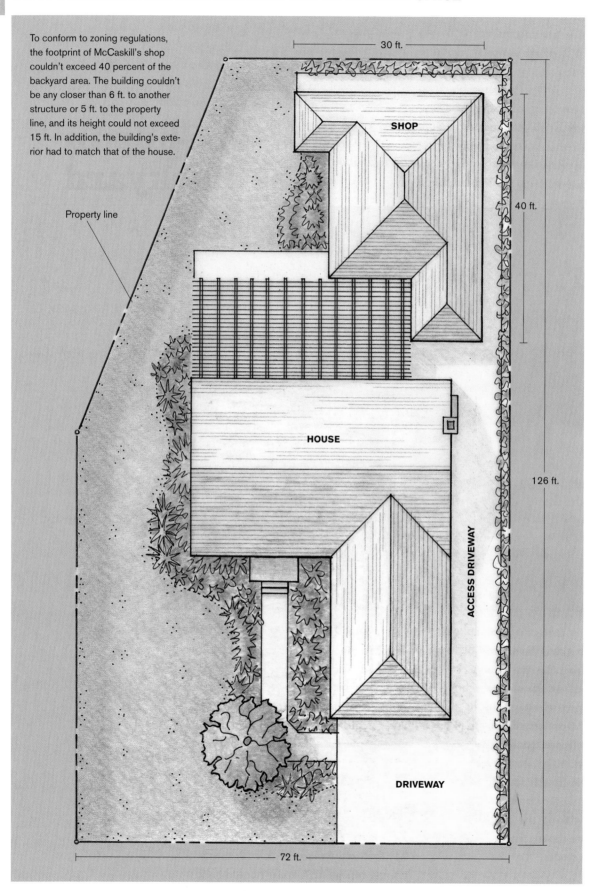

Property line

30 ft.

40 ft.

SHOP

HOUSE

126 ft.

ACCESS DRIVEWAY

DRIVEWAY

72 ft.

such a structure in our backyard. Their answer, in short, was no. However, a specific reason for the rejection was hard to get at, so I began asking more questions. Eventually, an inspector got involved, consulted the zoning restrictions, and he concluded that an accessory building would be okay as long as it didn't have a kitchen or bath.

The inspector's okay came with some limitations. The building footprint couldn't exceed 40 percent of the backyard area. Also, it could not be any closer than 6 ft. to a structure or 5 ft. to the property line. The building had to have an exterior that matched our house, and it couldn't exceed 15 ft. in height.

With these restrictions factored in, I determined I had room for a 940-sq.-ft. building. I then sketched a plot plan for the zoning officials to show both the house and workshop building. After their review, I had the zoning okay I needed.

Designing the Shop Building

Having cleared zoning, I started designing the shop. I purchased computer-aided design (CAD) software from Punch called Home Design Architectural Series (available at many home-electronics stores). It allowed me to design the building with relative ease.

Based on research and personal requirements, I concluded that the shop should have three rooms: one big and two small. The main shop room would have all the electrically powered machinery and tools. It also would house a long cutting bench for my radial-arm saw and miter saw. A smaller assembly room with a workbench, separate from the main room, also was important. So, too, was a small storage room to contain some of the especially noisy equipment, like the vacuum system and air compressor.

The cutting bench extends nearly the full length of a 40-ft.-long wall so that I can easily crosscut long boards. To make efficient use of space, my design included

storage underneath the bench. And because the wall was windowless, I added a bank of cabinets above the bench.

I determined that the assembly room would work nicely just off the west end of the patio. That location allowed for a 5-ft.-wide sliding door that opens to an access driveway, making it convenient to bring wood in and finished furniture out.

The next key item was lots of power, both 115v and 220v. Because I was pulling the main power off my existing home, I had 100 amps available for the shop. That was enough to allow multiple circuits, including one for each of my heavy, power-consuming tools.

To provide clearance when working with long boards or 4-ft. by 8-ft. sheet goods, I wanted a 10-ft.-high ceiling. Also, I didn't want support posts in the open area of the shop, as posts always seem to get in the way. But it took some extra planning to meet those two requirements. Indeed, I had to get some help from a structural engineer. We devised a gable-roof design using two 25-ft.-long, 8-in. by 14-in. solid-wood

STARTING SMALL. A scale model, with a removable roof, provided a useful three-dimensional view of the shop plan.

A WIDE-OPEN FLOOR PLAN. Engineered beams eliminate the need for support posts that take up space and get in the way. The entire shop floor is covered with interlocking rubber mats that are easy on the feet.

Storage room

Sander

Workbench

Lathe

Cutting bench

Revolving machine stand

Miter saw

Band-saw

Drum sander

Radial-arm saw

Tablesaw

Jointer

Drill press

Board and plywood storage

Assembly bench

Sliding door

beams, each weighing 1,000 lb. The result is an attractive open-beam look.

With the floor plan worked out, I was ready to tackle the placement of the machines, an important step because it would define where I should place the electrical components and the drops for the air compressor and vacuum system. The CAD software made it easy to add scaled-down drawings of the machines and to move them around the floor plan until I was satisfied there was adequate access to each one.

To make sure I was correct, though, I wanted to have a 3D view of the building. So, using foamboard, I built a scale model of the shop, including the cutting bench and machines. Looking at the model allowed me to foresee that the large beams were going to create problems with the windows, skylights, machinery placement, and sliding door. Working with the model proved to be time well spent, as it is much easier to change foamboard than wood.

The last of the planning focused on making the shop comfortable. I wanted to

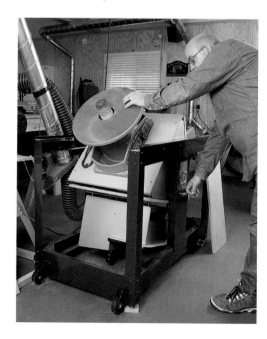

SPACE-SAVING STAND. A Sears®/Craftsman® revolving workstation holds three benchtop machines: a spindle sander, a benchtop planer, and a pocket-hole cutter.

have as much natural light as possible, so windows and skylights were important. I included in my design five large, energy-efficient, low-E, low-noise windows along with four skylights. I also included a 2-ton central heating and air-conditioning system, a practical addition in Southern California. Because I spend a lot of time in the shop, I also installed a 19-in. television, a DVD player and VCR, and a surround-sound speaker system.

To reduce the use of air conditioning, I planned for five ceiling fans. For additional energy efficiency and to diminish the amount of machine noise getting out into the neighborhood, I installed extra insulation—R30 value in the ceiling and R13 in the walls. Last, I decided to make the floor more comfortable by covering it with interlocking ⅝-in.-thick by 2-ft.-square rubber mats. The mats also are friendlier on dropped tools.

For safety, I wanted all of the electrical outlets to have ground-fault circuit interrupters (GFCI). This device recognizes when current has escaped from its intended circuit and instantaneously shuts off any further current flow. And although not required by code, an overhead sprinkler system was installed to provide added peace of mind.

In addition, I included a 2-hp dust-collection system with a 1-micron filter, one that automatically activates the vacuum and gates when a machine is turned on. Steel ducts eliminate any static discharge, and dust missed by the collection system is picked up by a ceiling-mounted air cleaner, also with a 1-micron filter.

Construction Went Smoothly

The contractor and city officials accepted my CAD drawings, so there was no need to hire an architect, a savings of about $5,000. I also saved about $35,000 by doing much of the work myself. Contractors were used only to build the cement foundation, the

CONVENIENT ACCESS. An auxiliary driveway along one side of the house leads to a wide sliding door at the shop, so wood can be brought in and finished furniture can be removed with a minimum of hassle.

exterior structure, and the roof; to install the heating and air conditioning; and to bring in the main power.

I had no problem doing the electrical, plumbing, and finishing work. From start to finish, the shop construction took about five and a half months. For the ceiling, I decided on drywall, painted white for added brightness. Beadboard-plywood interior walls provide a warm wood look that goes nicely with the wood beams in the cathedral. It's also a good surface for mounting cabinets and hanging tools.

Sticking to my original budget was tough, but I managed to keep it close. The total construction cost of the shop was about $83,000, less the tools, benches, and cabinets that I moved from the garage. A not-so-small side benefit: My wife and I now have plenty of room to park both of our cars in the garage.

RICK McCASKILL has been a woodworker for more than 35 years.

A Shop Inspired by School Memories

BY MARK BELLONBY

My introduction to woodworking took place in a high school arts building during the late 1960s. The building included a large, first-floor woodshop with a high ceiling and tall, Gothic windows that provided plenty of natural light and cross ventilation.

Space between machines and benches in the shop was plentiful, and the tools were stored in beautiful, enclosed oak cabinets. Eventually, I had a key to the building, and I sometimes would work until the early hours of the morning, completely lost in the craft of making furniture.

That bright and airy school shop became the standard against which all of my later shops were measured. For many years, I had little choice but to cope with workshops located in dark, dusty, and confined basements or garages. I hoped someday to have a workplace that offered the many advantages of that wonderful school shop.

Must-Have Design Considerations

Two years ago, I finally got the opportunity to design my own freestanding shop. The obvious deficiencies I'd put up with for so long made it easy to come up with a list of goals for the new space.

An architect by profession, I produced the design and drawings using a computer-aided design (CAD) system. The builder, Martin Jarvis, helped keep costs in line, and he was frequently consulted during the design process. He encouraged me to consider a simple building shape and to use standard windows and skylights. He also helped me find cost-effective materials, like the base-grade, strip-oak flooring I ended up using.

To allow room for machinery and work in process, it was most important for me to have a generous amount of floor space. High ceilings were a priority, and the floor plan had to be flexible to allow for rearranging machines.

Like my school shop, I wanted mine to be bright and airy, almost an extension

of the outside. Evenly distributed natural light was going to be critical to the design, as well as excellent ventilation. That meant the shop had to have large windows and skylights, all located to provide maximum light and quick air changes.

Several other design objectives also were important. I wanted to minimize noise from the air compressor and dust-collection system. Also, the building had to be energy efficient. And, should the need ever arise, I wanted a building that could be converted to an alternate use with relative ease.

A separate finishing room would have been nice, but I figured it would take up too much space. At some point in the future, a nearby outbuilding has the potential to become a finishing room.

A Smart, Flexible Floor Plan

Using a scale model for guidance, I sited the shop 20 ft. from an existing farm outbuilding. That allowed me to use part of the outbuilding for storage. A concrete slab between the two buildings is easily accessed through large doors in each building. This small courtyard is protected somewhat by the buildings and nearby trees, and I often use the area to plane or sand when I want to enjoy the outdoors or keep messy operations out of the workshop. Also, in an open area against one of the walls, I included a deep sink that's handy for cleanup of all sorts.

Separate Work Zones in the Shop Room

Using the CAD computer software, I placed drawings of each machine onto the floor plan

Planning Pays Off

In designing his dream workshop, Bellonby placed a premium on having lots of light, ventilation, and elbow room. Equally important, however, was having work zones arranged in a logical fashion.

DESIGN ROOM OFFERS ADDITIONAL WORKSPACE. The large desk in the office is a perfect surface for laying out veneer.

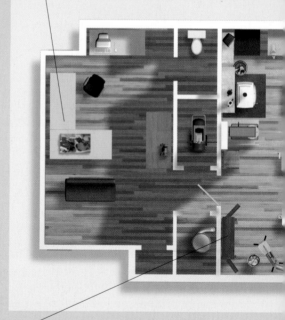

TOOLS WITHIN EASY REACH. A freestanding hand-tool cabinet occupies a corner of the shop not far from the workbench.

DIVIDER ADDS STORAGE. A freestanding partition provides a sturdy wall for storing tools and accessories, and the shelves can be used for wood storage.

WORKBENCH IS CENTRALLY LOCATED. The most convenient location for the workbench proved to be approximately in the middle of the shop.

CONVERTING STATIONARY TO PORTABLE. Several tools can be moved around the shop on shopmade mobile bases.

of the shop room and moved them around. I considered a number of arrangements before finding one that looked best. This process proved most helpful when it came time to add the real machinery to the shop. However, in the course of using the shop for about a year, I have occasionally reshuffled the machines to fine-tune the layout.

The shop machinery is organized into four general work zones: two machine-tool areas, a hand-tool area, and an assembly area. Because the shop room is a relatively small area, most of the machines are on shopmade mobile bases so that they can be moved around to create more floor area as needed. The heavy tools, however, like the tablesaw, wood lathe, and metalworking lathe, are stationary.

Wood and Wood Storage

Wood-storage areas often take up a lot of space. They also provide an attractive habitat for all kinds of animals and insects. To minimize such problems, I put my lumber racks, sheet-good storage, and veneer-storage crates in the adjacent outbuilding, along with a 12-in. sliding miter saw for cutting boards to rough length.

Solid wood goes into the shop as it is needed. So only a limited amount of wood is stored in the main building. Full-size plywood and other sheet goods are either cut to rough size in the courtyard or run through the tablesaw. In the future they will be done on a panel saw I plan to add in the outbuilding.

Convenient Accessories

I arranged floor-mounted dust-collection ports and power outlets adjacent to each other, creating a series of utility stations of sorts. Whenever possible, I tried to locate the stations in areas that always would be likely places to put machinery, even if it all was rearranged some day. In general, this approach has worked out pretty well, although the stations can become obstacles when machinery is wheeled out of the way.

ONE SHOP, TWO WORKSPACES

The two primary areas of the building are a shop room to the west and a design/multipurpose room to the east. Between them are a small bathroom and two closets—one housing the air compressor and one containing the dust-collection system. Because the compressor and dust collector are enclosed, Bellonby hears just enough noise to know that they're running.

Dust collection
A central dust-collection system was designed with help from Oneida Air Systems. Starting the collector simply is a matter of opening the blast gate at the machine and then using a remote-control switch to start the system. The ducts run under the floor in the crawl space.

The compressed-air system was designed to include a port within 20 ft. of each machine. A port also is located at the dust collector and outside the building in the courtyard. That outside port gets a lot of use, as I prefer working alfresco for certain woodworking tasks, such as sanding. All of the pipes slope to a drain in the crawl space. It's important for the pipes to slope, because any water that collects at a low spot can wreak havoc with certain air tools.

The generous upper wall spaces, courtesy of the cathedral ceiling, are good places to put speaker mounts. And a television on a high shelf is welcomed at break time.

MARK BELLONBY is an architect and woodworker living in northern Virginia.

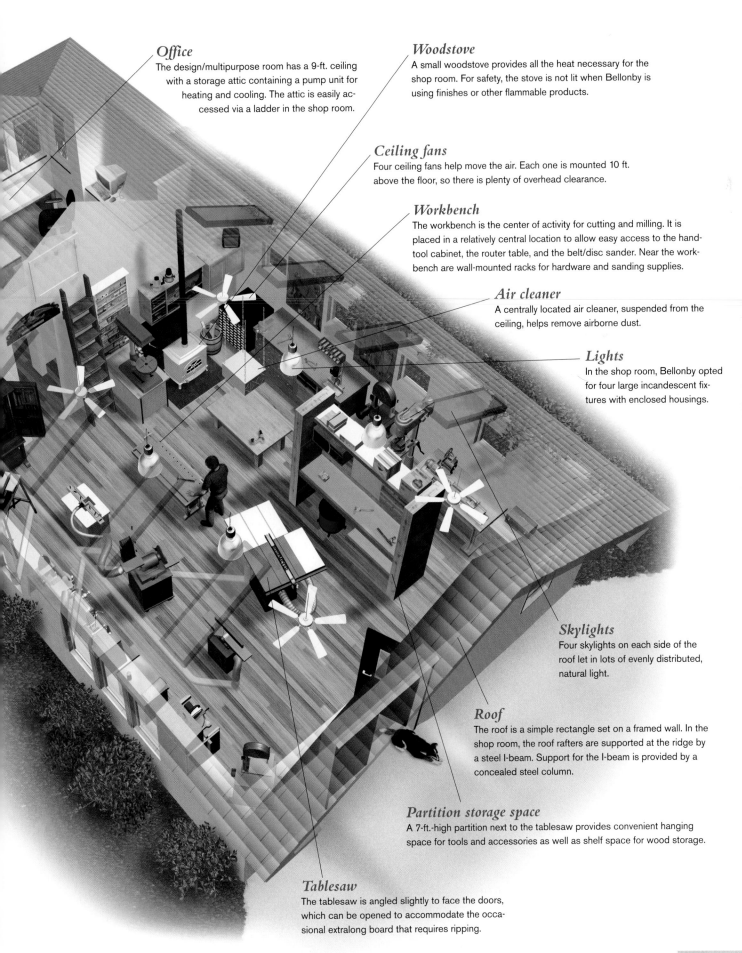

Office
The design/multipurpose room has a 9-ft. ceiling with a storage attic containing a pump unit for heating and cooling. The attic is easily accessed via a ladder in the shop room.

Woodstove
A small woodstove provides all the heat necessary for the shop room. For safety, the stove is not lit when Bellonby is using finishes or other flammable products.

Ceiling fans
Four ceiling fans help move the air. Each one is mounted 10 ft. above the floor, so there is plenty of overhead clearance.

Workbench
The workbench is the center of activity for cutting and milling. It is placed in a relatively central location to allow easy access to the hand-tool cabinet, the router table, and the belt/disc sander. Near the workbench are wall-mounted racks for hardware and sanding supplies.

Air cleaner
A centrally located air cleaner, suspended from the ceiling, helps remove airborne dust.

Lights
In the shop room, Bellonby opted for four large incandescent fixtures with enclosed housings.

Skylights
Four skylights on each side of the roof let in lots of evenly distributed, natural light.

Roof
The roof is a simple rectangle set on a framed wall. In the shop room, the roof rafters are supported at the ridge by a steel I-beam. Support for the I-beam is provided by a concealed steel column.

Partition storage space
A 7-ft.-high partition next to the tablesaw provides convenient hanging space for tools and accessories as well as shelf space for wood storage.

Tablesaw
The tablesaw is angled slightly to face the doors, which can be opened to accommodate the occasional extralong board that requires ripping.

From the Ground Up

BY WILLIAM DUCKWORTH

Nowadays I make a living with words, not wood, but for the better part of two decades I worked full time as a cabinetmaker. Along the way I had five different shops, two of them in basements. To be kind, I'd characterize those basement shops as less than ideal—there was not much light, not much air circulation, and not much headroom. One had a river running through it every time it rained. So when my wife and I built an addition to our house recently and decided that the new basement was the place for my shop, I was determined to steer clear of those miseries.

If you are planning to include a basement shop in a new house, an addition, or an existing space, you might benefit from my experience. I found that by attending to a few key design considerations you can make a sweet shop in a subterranean setting. One important note before I begin: Whether or not you are working with an architect, it's best to address all of your concerns before the drawings are done. Making changes after construction begins is needlessly expensive.

The Floor Plan: Strive to Keep it Open

One of my old shops was in a post-and-beam building with a grid of support columns cluttering the floor space every 8 ft. The posts limited the placement of machinery, interfered with work flow, and drove me mad.

When my wife and I designed our addition, we decided to avoid the encumbrance of posts or load-bearing walls by carrying the load from the floor above

THE WELL-CONSIDERED BASEMENT SHOP

Drywall over the plywood brings the fire rating up to code.

Lightweight foam blocks quickly snap together to create the forms for poured concrete walls. The blocks stay in place after the pour, providing high R-value insulation.

I-beam eliminates need for posts, creating an open floor plan.

A layer of plywood makes for easy mounting of cabinets, tool racks, and jigs on every inch of wall space.

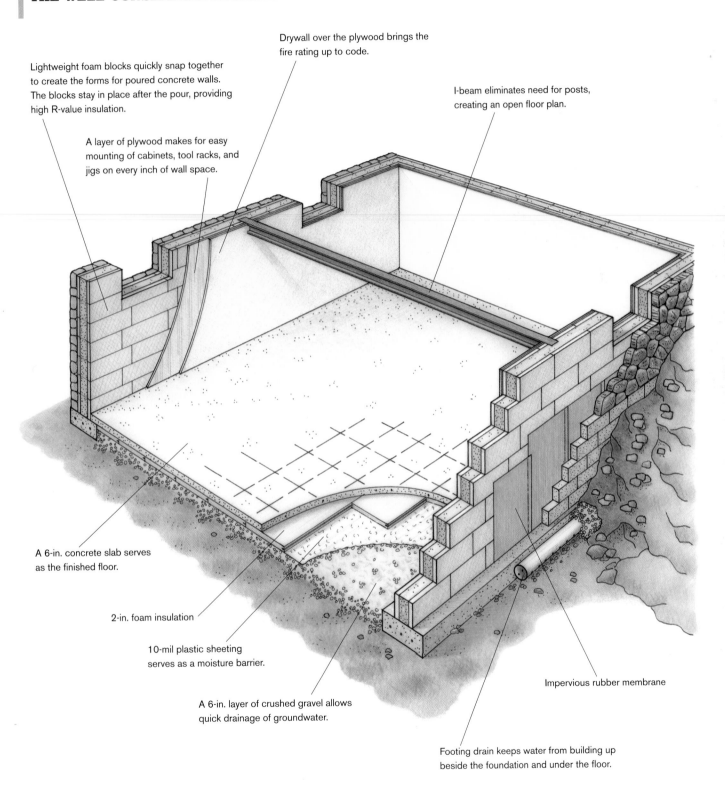

A 6-in. concrete slab serves as the finished floor.

2-in. foam insulation

10-mil plastic sheeting serves as a moisture barrier.

A 6-in. layer of crushed gravel allows quick drainage of groundwater.

Impervious rubber membrane

Footing drain keeps water from building up beside the foundation and under the floor.

WITHIN. Glazed doors and a half
dozen small windows fill the
east-facing basement shop with
daylight. High-output fluorescents carry the load at night and
help balance the light during
the day.

with a steel I-beam. My wife is an architect,
but we consulted an engineer to size the
beam. We also had to work out the details
of how it should tie into the concrete
foundation walls and fabricate the forms
accordingly. The beam was surprisingly
affordable, and it provided a convenient
mount for a hoist to lift heavy machines.

Water Is the Enemy: Keep the Space Dry

Having suffered the indignity of rusted
tools in that riverine basement shop, I was
determined to guarantee a bone-dry space.
After the hole for the new basement was
dug, I was taken aback by how much water ran steadily underground. Because our
house is on a hill, the solution was a footing drain made from perforated 4-in. PVC
pipe bedded in gravel that drains downhill
to daylight. For a house on flat terrain, you
might need a sump pump.

To keep water from seeping through the
foundation walls, I applied a heavy-duty,
self-stick rubber membrane on the exterior
before the walls were covered with a stone
veneer and backfilled. The 39-in.-wide
membrane strips are applied vertically with
a 3-in. overlap. Each strip begins slightly
above grade and runs down to the base of
the footing, covering the seam between
the wall and the footing. This stuff wasn't
cheap, but I'm convinced that it will hold
up longer and provide a more impervious
moisture barrier than a layer of tar.

Before the floor slab was poured, I put
down a 10-mil plastic moisture barrier. As
soon as the concrete was firm enough to
walk on, I applied a waterproof treatment.
Overkill? Maybe, but it's been several years,
and I haven't glimpsed the slightest hint of
moisture in the space.

Doors: Easy Access Is Critical

I've accumulated a collection of fairly large woodworking machines, so generous access to my shop was a necessity. Given that our addition was going on the downhill side of the slope we live on, it was a no-brainer that we'd build a walk-out basement. We installed double doors, which provide an opening that is 68 in. wide. If you're limited to one door, I'd recommend a minimum 36-in.-wide opening.

If your property won't allow a walk-out basement, Bilco® doors may be the next best way to avoid dragging equipment and lumber through the house.

Light: You Need a Lot

The glass doors we chose for the shop do wonders for lighting the space during the day. Even the six small windows I put in help in that regard (and provide cross-ventilation).

I installed fluorescent fixtures, which provide even lighting at a low cost. I chose standard industrial strips with 8-ft.-long, high-output lamps. I painted the walls and storage cabinets white to enhance the reflected light in the room.

Ceilings: Higher Is Better

Having worked in basements with 7-ft. ceilings, I'm especially sensitive to the grief low ceilings can cause when handling long planks or sheets of plywood. Our original plan called for a 10-ft. clearance between the finished floor and the underside of the joists to the floor above. But we lost a foot when the excavator hit hardpan. Still, I had a 9-ft. clearance, which is ample. A standard 8-ft. ceiling would have been workable, but the extra foot not only makes material handling easier, it also gives my shop nearly 100 extra square feet of wall space for storage.

AMPLE ACCESS FROM OUTDOORS. Double doors on Duckworth's walk-out basement make it easy to move in machines and materials and to carry out finished work.

Electricity: Don't Skimp on the Power

I did most of the wiring for my shop myself, but hired an electrician to bring in a 100-amp subpanel, which is more than enough power for what I need. I used the brand-name circuit breakers that the panel manufacturer recommended.

In our area, the electrical code states that receptacles are to be placed so that no point on the wall is more than 6 ft. from an outlet. I installed mine every 5 ft. and put in 20-amp circuits, using no. 12 wire in metallic-coated cable. In addition to the regular receptacles, I put in one 220v receptacle for my dust collector and another 220v circuit for my three-phase converter.

I wired the lights on two different circuits: In the unlikely event that one of them blows, I won't be fumbling in the dark to see where I'm going.

WILLIAM DUCKWORTH is a *Fine Woodworking* contributing editor, writer, and professional woodworker in western Connecticut.

By attending to a few key design considerations, you can make a sweet shop in a subterranean setting.

Dream Shop
in the Woods

BY LES CIZEK

The first impression people get when they enter our shop is that it looks more like a gallery than a shop. With artwork, large workspaces, whimsical design details, and shining, clean floors, our shop is not like the cozy dens that many woodworkers use. It is, however, an efficient and comfortable place to work. As full-time custom furniture makers, my business partner Harry Van Ornum and I use every square foot of our shop, called Four Sisters Woodworking (inspired by a quirky Victorian photograph).

We've designed the space to be large, open, and light-filled because that's the kind of environment we like to work in. Our shop is also the culmination of lessons learned from the poorly made shops we've worked in over the years.

Separate Rooms for Bench Work and Machine Work

Because the furniture makers spend 80 percent of their time in the bench room, they relegated machine and bench work to separate rooms, giving each partner a quieter place for hand-tool work.

BENCH ROOM

BENCH ROOM FOR TWO. With high ceilings and lots of light, the bench room is a comfortable place for handwork and finishing.

MACHINE ROOM

EFFICIENT LAYOUT. Machines are arranged so that wood progresses in logical order from the lumber rack through all of the workstations.

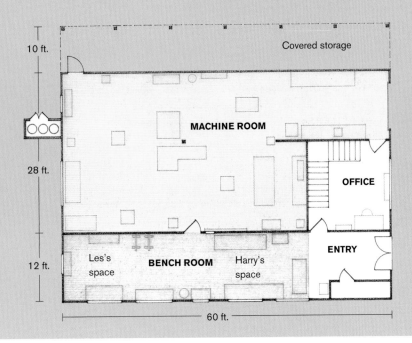

Harry's Bench Space

Harry Van Ornum's furniture requires a lot of handwork, and he does most of his work at his bench. He keeps frequently used tools nearby, such as clamps, squares, and planes. He admits that he has more planes than he uses, but as a collector as well as a user, he sees them as functional art.

CUTTING TOOLS IN LINE. On his other bench (across from the planes), Van Ornum keeps his chisels and carving gouges within easy reach.

Les's Bench Space

Cizek's fiery-faced tool cabinet in the background is typical of his finishing style, which frequently incorporates bright colors. His work area has the requisite shaping tools and a workbench.

A TEMPLE FOR TOOLS. Cizek decided that his prized, and much-used, custom Japanese spokeshaves needed to have their own home.

KEEPING THOSE SMALL PARTS ORGANIZED. Cizek made a library-card-catalog-style chest for screws, hardware, and other items.

Harry and I have more than 40 years of woodworking experience between us. We started our partnership in 1995 in a leased space in downtown Fort Bragg, Calif. We ran that shop for five years, renting bench space to four other woodworkers. It got to be a very busy place, and Harry and I found we were doing a lot of things other than making furniture. We decided to sell the place and build a perfect shop just for the two of us, leaving the landlord hassle behind.

This new shop is a unique and functional workspace (see the floor plan on p. 73). It comes very close to fulfilling our vision of the perfect shop.

Learning from Our Old Shops

Years ago, I had my first shop in Florida in a corner of a storage building that was used primarily to shelter a boat. The space was cramped and dirty and left little room to work. Next came a garage with an awning that enabled me to move my work outside on good days. Harry also had some very poor shop spaces, the most notable being an unheated space in Minnesota.

The common denominator of all those shops seemed to be that none of them were designed for, or dedicated to, woodworking. We made buildings into woodworking shops rather than designed a shop just for woodworking.

Our ideal shop would have plenty of natural light, easy access for large pieces of lumber and sheet goods to be brought in, appropriate wiring for three-phase and single-phase machines, and, finally, a comfortable floor.

As Harry and I sat down to plan our new shop, we knew we wanted to build a woodworking space from the ground up.

The Building Blends with the Site

Harry and his wife, Scotty Lyons, own a forested five-acre site about a mile from downtown Fort Bragg, and we decided to build there. We sited the shop to appear as if it were emerging from the woods. Warm and inviting, the building fits naturally into the surrounding redwood forest.

The exterior is typical of Mendocino County barns. The footprint is 60 ft. by 50 ft., which includes a 10-ft. by 60-ft. unenclosed extension on the south side. Harry's wife has a weaving studio in the upstairs portion of the shop, which is about 650 sq. ft. The basic shell of the building was erected by a contractor who specializes in agricultural and warehouse construction. Harry and I installed the windows and finished the interior, including building the second floor and all of the walls. Harry is also a general contractor, and his skills and knowledge made this work go smoothly.

The unenclosed storage area runs the full length of the building. Eventually, we'd like to enclose this area, but for now it's where we keep rough lumber as well as our panel saw for cutting large sheet materials.

The shop's exterior is redwood board and batten, and the roof is steel painted dark green. Sixteen skylights pierce the roof and produce a strong, diffuse light through the interior.

Separating Bench and Machine Rooms

One major influence on our shop's design was the shop at the College of the Redwoods, which we both attended. The shop boasts separate bench and machine rooms. The advantage of this setup is that noise and dust are confined to the machine room, leaving the bench room as a quiet retreat for more intense work. The wall between these rooms has a layer of insulation and sound channel to help keep things quiet. While one of us is working stock in the machine room, the other can be cutting dovetails or drawing in the bench room. Neither disturbs the other.

The Machine Room

ROUGH LUMBER ENTERS HERE. The lumber rack is close to the chopsaw. The jointer and planer are stationed just beyond.

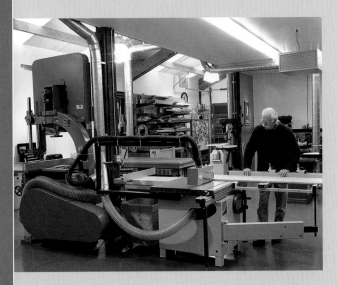

DUST COLLECTION FOR LARGE MACHINES. The 36-in. bandsaw and sliding tablesaw are grouped together so that they can share a duct for efficient dust collection.

WORKSHOP ZONES

Each operation has a zone within the shop at Four Sisters Woodworking. Lumber enters through the large garage-style door and then makes its way through milling, shaping, and eventually to the bench room for handwork and finishing.

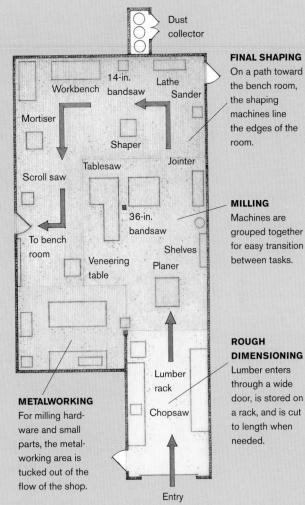

Dust collector

FINAL SHAPING
On a path toward the bench room, the shaping machines line the edges of the room.

MILLING
Machines are grouped together for easy transition between tasks.

ROUGH DIMENSIONING
Lumber enters through a wide door, is stored on a rack, and is cut to length when needed.

METALWORKING
For milling hardware and small parts, the metalworking area is tucked out of the flow of the shop.

Workbench
14-in. bandsaw
Lathe
Sander
Mortiser
Shaper
Jointer
Tablesaw
Scroll saw
36-in. bandsaw
Shelves
Planer
To bench room
Veneering table
Lumber rack
Chopsaw
Entry

The 12-ft. by 60-ft. bench room occupies the north side of the building. It is lit by six skylights, five north-facing windows, and three metal halide lamps. Because we spend most of our time in the bench room, we tried to make it comfortable, with lots of colors, painted wood floors, and framed prints on the walls. We have found that being surrounded by color and art influences the creative process in each of us.

Likewise, the number of windows adds to the pleasing atmosphere. Whimsically shaped, recycled windows let in light between the rooms and break the expanse of large, white wall.

The machine room is accessed through a 3½-ft.-wide, two-way swinging door. The floor is a concrete slab painted with a durable epoxy paint. We left plenty of room around each machine to make the movement of stock easier. The machine room is lit by a combination of fluorescent lights and 10 skylights. With the skylights, we don't have to turn on the fluorescents until the evening.

Here on the north coast of California, summertime highs reach only the 60s and winters can be cold and damp. So we installed radiant heat under the floor in the bench room and placed forced-air propane heaters in the machine room.

How the Shop Works

In the machine room, we designed our shop around the flow of rough lumber to finished furniture. On the right side of the shop through a large garage door, we unload our lumber to the storage rack. We currently have a small lumber-storage rack where we keep a collection of furniture-grade wood (we keep a large cache in a barn at Harry's house). From there, we can take the lumber directly to the planer for milling. The jointer and large bandsaw are beyond the planer for

While one of us is working stock in the machine room, the other can be cutting dovetails or drawing in the bench room. Neither disturbs the other.

further dimensioning. Next to the bandsaw, we have a sliding tablesaw for sheet goods and other uses. On the perimeter, we've located the shaping tools, such as a lathe, shaper, and sanding machines, because they are used primarily with smaller pieces and don't require the room needed for manipulating large lumber. But we've left plenty of space between machines so that we can move around easily.

Harry and I do a lot of veneering, so we set up the bandsaw, jointer, and veneering table for this process. We placed the jointer next to the large bandsaw, because while we're cutting veneers we often like to joint a face in order to get a clean cut.

We also have a metalworking area where we mill custom parts and hardware. We tucked this part of the shop into a corner of the machine room so that metal filings are kept away from lumber.

Our central dust-collection system is a three-phase, 7½-hp unit. We routed the ducting to each machine. The dust collector is outside the shop on the east side to keep the noise away.

Each of our bench spaces reflects our personal interests. I use a wide variety of finishes, including aniline dyes, so my tool cabinet has a fiery red face. I also have a cabinet full of my most-used finishing supplies and I am able to get to what I need easily. In addition, I have the hand tools that I require, but not much more. I do have a special set of Japanese spokeshaves that were custom made. To honor them as well as their maker, I built a small wall-hung pagoda that houses them.

Harry is a collector and user of old tools, so around his bench he has a variety of classic, old planes. He also is an accomplished carver; therefore, his gouges and chisels are laid out in a line for easy access.

In addition to the natural and artificial light overhead, we installed spotlights at our work areas. We do all of our finishing at our benches. Because we use mostly rub-on finishes, we have no need for a spray booth, and the bench room is adequate for this work.

For the most part, this shop fulfills our dreams. Although we wouldn't say that it has changed our furniture, a pleasant shop does make it easier to create quality work. In fact, we believe that our design of a large, open, and light-filled space reflects the philosophy of our shop motto: *Sat cito, si sat bene* (Soon enough, if done well). If we were to start over, the only thing we'd change, believe it or not, is to make the shop larger.

LES CIZEK builds custom furniture in Fort Bragg, California. His wife, Norma Watkins, assisted with the chapter.

A COLORFUL CLAMP RACK. The colors throughout the shop brighten the environment. The clamp rack also provides a reliable spot for storing essential tools. Portholes in the swinging door help avoid head-on collisions.

A Timber-Frame Dream

BY ERIC FOERTSCH

For 15 years I dreamed of building the perfect shop. After making do with space in cramped, dark garages and basements, I wanted a workspace that was bright and inspiring. When we moved from New York to Connecticut, I had my chance.

Designing my ideal shop building consumed the first few months of 2004. I made lists, read books and magazines, drew on 15 years of experience, and made dozens of layouts on graph paper.

I kept asking myself if the shop building would create a positive, a neutral, or a negative value for the property. In the end, I decided that a building made with conventional framing would be a neutral addition at best, but a properly executed timber-frame structure would be a positive—especially from inside, where it

IT JUST LOOKS OLD. This 24-ft. by 36-ft. shop dates from mid-2005. It was made to resemble a 19th-century barn, using post-and-beam construction. Inside, the massive timbers dominate. Arranging the tablesaw island and other machines for maximum efficiency took weeks of planning.

OLD TIMBERS, MODERN SKIN

In a typical timber-frame structure, vertical posts, horizontal beams, and rafters are fastened together on the ground to make an assembly known as a bent. The bents are then hoisted upright and tied together with horizontal members called girts. Here, the contractors added rafters after raising the bents. This age-old timber frame skeleton is sheathed and insulated with modern materials.

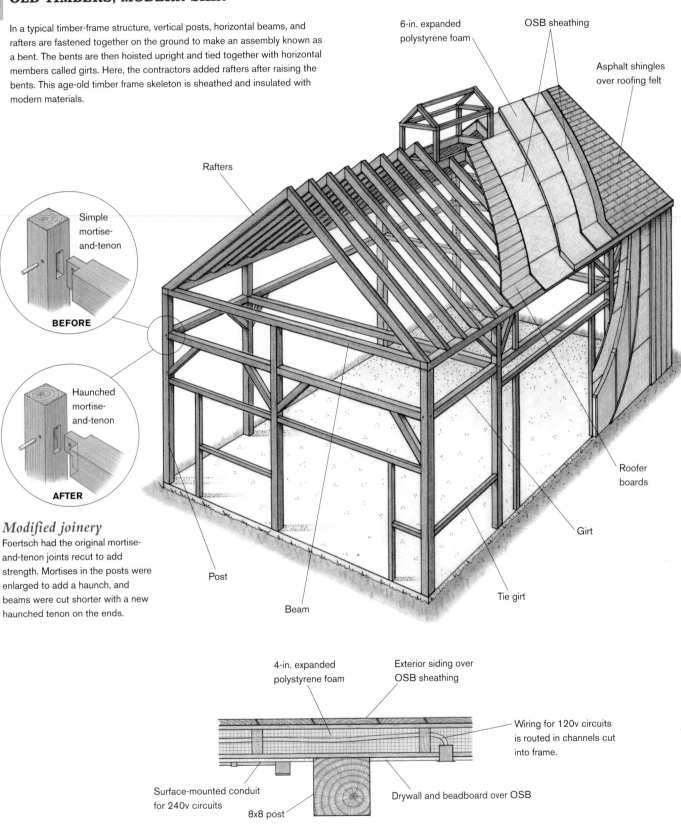

Simple mortise-and-tenon

BEFORE

Haunched mortise-and-tenon

AFTER

Modified joinery
Foertsch had the original mortise-and-tenon joints recut to add strength. Mortises in the posts were enlarged to add a haunch, and beams were cut shorter with a new haunched tenon on the ends.

6-in. expanded polystyrene foam

OSB sheathing

Asphalt shingles over roofing felt

Rafters

Roofer boards

Girt

Tie girt

Post

Beam

4-in. expanded polystyrene foam

Exterior siding over OSB sheathing

Wiring for 120v circuits is routed in channels cut into frame.

Surface-mounted conduit for 240v circuits

8x8 post

Drywall and beadboard over OSB

Wall Detail

would be obvious that this was no ordinary structure. A timber-frame shop also would fit in with the neighborhood and would be adaptable for other uses.

Hardwood floors, wainscoting, and finished walls between the exposed post-and-beam structure give the shop the bright and inspiring appearance I've craved. If the next owner doesn't need a shop, the building will work as office space or as a studio.

In my experience, building a timber-frame structure involves about as much time and expense as a conventional stick-frame building. The biggest drawback to timber framing is the extra time needed to get building permits and find a reputable, affordable timber framer. Timber framers don't use graded lumber, so a building inspector may require a structural engineer to provide a set of plans that include all the necessary load and span calculations.

Setback requirements for local zoning restricted me to a 24-ft. by 36-ft. structure. With its second-floor loft, the building has 1,500 sq. ft. of floor space. That's large enough to satisfy my main requirement: being able to work with plywood sheets anywhere in the shop. Still, I couldn't make space for a finishing room or a dedicated place to dry wood.

Before I could proceed, I had to gain the building inspector's approval. I used Tedd Benson's book *Building the Timber Frame House* (Fireside, 1981) to provide tables, charts, and stress calculations for every joint and beam. It helped to over-engineer the design. If you're not up to dealing with the local building department, be sure that the timber-framing contractor you hire can obtain needed permits and variances.

Getting Real

Internet research turned up companies that would build a brand-new timber frame, but they were way too expensive—about $45,000 just for materials. That's three times

LOTS OF STORAGE. **The shop has more than 20 ft. of drawers and cabinets along one wall (see the photo above), with more built into the workbench and tablesaw island. Upstairs, a loft provides ample storage for wood and assorted odds and ends (see the photo on the facing page).**

the cost of conventional stick framing. My best option seemed to be a company that could dismantle, repair, and reassemble a timber frame on my property. Their prices came closest to fitting my budget.

That led me to Jesse Benedict of Benedict Antique Lumber and Stone, in New Milford, Pa. Benedict had a hundred-year-old barn that could be modified to meet my needs by cutting a foot off each main beam. And, to stay on the good side of the building inspector, I had Benedict recut the post-and-beam joints to make them haunched mortises, thereby strengthening each joint.

Barn Raising

In early May, Benedict and his four-man crew arrived with a flatbed truck hauling the components for the basic frame. Rafters, roofing lumber, and sheathing filled another two trucks.

The men raised each of the 1,000-lb. post-and-beam assemblies (known as bents) by hand, pulling it upright with ropes. Then, balancing themselves on the 8-in.-wide beams like trapeze artists, they attached the rafters. That part of the barn raising took them only three days; they needed another month to sheathe the walls and roof with plywood, oriented strand board, and rigid foam. Over the rough sheathing on the interior, I attached beadboard wainscot panels 4 ft. high. A large beam called a tie girt hides the seam between the beadboard and the wallboard that runs to the ceiling.

The shop cost me about $35,000 in all, about what a comparable conventional building would cost in my area.

Finishing Touches

I didn't limit my recycling to the post-and-beam structure. The 11 double-hung win-dows came from a contractor tearing down a nearby house. Windows in the roof cupola are salvaged French doors turned sideways. The beech hardwood floor came from a company auctioning offcuts and seconds online. I also turned to the Internet for the porcelain barn lamps that supply most of the lighting.

I still have to finish the second-story loft and add window trim and a few other details. But from the outside, the building looks just like a 19th-century barn. And my wife says the space inside is already nicer than our house.

ERIC FOERTSCH is a self-taught weekend wood-worker. He picked up the pastime 14 years ago, and uses it as an outlet to unwind from his full-time technology consulting business.

A Workshop Steeped in History

BY EUGENE LANDON

When someone enters my shop, invariably they feel as if they've stepped back in time. The walls are lined with antique hand tools, the floor is made from wide pine boards, and period furniture pieces are all around in various stages of construction or repair. Visitors who are woodworkers are the first to notice the modern chopsaw, the tablesaw, and, upon closer investigation, a nearly buried heavy-duty thickness planer. Their reaction is sometimes relief: "He's one of us after all—he does use power tools."

I'd be the first to admit that I have a serious tool-collecting habit. Like all collectors, I love the anticipation of attending an auction or tag sale and finding an heirloom tool. My favorite old tools are a rosewood marking gauge and a ½-in. Marples chisel with a boxwood handle. When I discovered a few years ago that this model was being discontinued, I quickly bought several more so that I'd have a lifetime supply. My most valuable tool is probably one of my 19th-century plow planes.

Unlike pure collectors, I still use my old tools; that's how I justify my huge collection. All molding is done with a combination of molding planes and carving tools, so, not surprisingly, I have large collections of both. Most woodworkers are taught to make the

EIGHTEENTH-CENTURY SHOP LIVES IN THE 21ST CENTURY. Though only antique hand tools are readily visible on the walls of his shop, Landon does employ modern machinery in his reproduction work.

HAND-TOOL HEAVEN. Landon justifies his huge collection of molding planes (above) by using them to cut all of his moldings. He also owns an extensive collection of carving tools for use on work such as this cartouche (top right) that will adorn the top of a secretary.

carving or molding fit the tool, but when you are making exact reproductions, it has to be the other way around.

There is one kind of hand tool that I believe is better new than old: Modern metal bench planes are infinitely superior to antique wooden ones. Both planes give an identical finish, but unlike wooden planes, metal planes aren't affected by changes in humidity. I don't have to waste time setting up a metal plane each time I use it.

Tools Are Stored for Convenience, Not for Display

When it comes to tool storage, each tool must be easily recognizable and readily available. If the tools look good lining the walls, so much the better. I don't keep anything locked away in display cases. And I prefer to store carving tools in drawers on a rolling cart so I can move them to where I need them.

A dozen drawers under my main workbench store tools, but most of the ones I use regularly are stored on a shelf behind the bench, and sometimes even on the bench. I don't believe in wasting time fetching and returning tools just for the sake of keeping the benchtop clear.

Some storage methods simply evolved after many years working in my shop. For example, I store my files in a cross section from a tree branch to keep them close at hand. I don't have to open a door or a drawer to get at them, and despite their numbers, I know the location of each one.

Several Benches Allow Working at an Optimal Height

When you are young, a comfortable place to work is a luxury; when you get to my age, it is a necessity. Most woodworkers' benches are too low. In the 18th century, all wood was planed from rough to finish by hand. But to plane away machine marks, less downward force is required, so it is more comfortable to work at a higher bench.

For carving, my Emmett patternmaker's vise is ideal. It can grasp odd-shaped work pieces and hold them at whatever angle is best for carving. I prefer to carve in natural light, so my benches are positioned to take advantage of light from the windows. Because my shop is deep in the woods, though, I usually end up using a desk lamp for extra light.

The top of my main workbench bears the scars from well over 30 years of use. I can see little point in having a pristine surface on a bench—the perfect wood surfaces leave the shop. I bought the bench used, added the storage drawers underneath, and raised the height to a more comfortable 36 in., which also matches the height of the carts in my shop.

Making an 18th-Century Masterpiece

What motivates me to come into this workshop each day? It certainly is not because I want to be remembered by posterity; none of my pieces are signed. In part, I am motivated by my love for this style of furniture. I admire the craftsmanship that went into the original pieces, and if in a century's time an expert can't tell my piece from an original, then I will be well pleased.

EUGENE LANDON makes 18th-century furniture near Williamsport, Pennsylvania.

No piece of furniture leaves my shop showing anything but the marks left by hand tools, even the insides of joints that never will see the light of day again. I also know, as any professional does, that time is money and that it pays to use power tools to make a piece as quickly as possible. Solving this contradiction—making reproduction furniture fast, and making it as faithful as possible—dominates the way I work.

A PLAN AND A RECORD OF EACH PIECE

Making faithful reproductions requires dead-accurate plans. I photograph, measure, and trace the carving of an original piece, then create templates for all of the components. When I'm finished, all of these documents are filed away should I ever need to build the same piece again.

I often wonder how an 18th-century woodworker might have tackled a problem. One technique I am particularly proud of is using rawhide as a template for making identical carvings.

I haven't found conclusive evidence that this method was followed in the 18th century, but the material was readily available, and I can't think of what else furniture makers back then would have used. Thin, damp rawhide is tightly bound around an existing carving and left for 24 hours. When the material dries, an impression remains. I cut away the surplus rawhide, leaving a perfect template, which I shellac to preserve. Using this method, I can lay out identical carvings on a set of chairs very quickly.

NATURE PREPARES MY LUMBER FOR MACHINING

A piece of furniture begins life behind my shop, where I air-dry thousands of board feet of hard- and softwood. I leave the stacks stickered and exposed year-round, which improves the color of the heartwood, although the sapwood rots. After two or three years, I dry the wood more in my electric kiln.

After I cut the boards to length, I joint and thickness them by machine, leaving about 1/16 in. in thickness to be removed with a handplane. Many 18th-century pieces were made from boards 2 ft. or 3 ft. wide, which I try to use where appropriate. Such magnificent boards, however, don't fit in my 16-in. planer. I take extrawide lumber to a large commercial shop that has a 48-in. planer.

THE BANDSAW AND LATHE TAKE OVER

Every cabriole leg starts out on my 20-in. bandsaw, a wonderful tool made by the American Saw Mill Machinery Co. and dating from goodness knows when. I use this machine far more than the tablesaw for cutting straight-grain sections from a board, multiple chair parts, and cabriole legs. I use only a ¼-in. blade. My 18th-century colleagues would have employed a bowsaw, but mine stays hanging on the wall.

My lathe, made by Hill, Clarke, and Co., has babbitt bearings and is at least 100 years old. I commonly turn finials, the feet of cabriole legs, and the quarter columns found on many period case pieces. Many woodworkers try to create these columns from a single piece of wood, which means they can't make through-flutes and must carve the end of each flute by hand. I copy the 18th-century woodworkers, who turned the bases and caps for an entire piece of furniture from one piece of wood, and then plowed the flutes with a no. 2 round molding plane before assembling the whole column.

Quick-to-Make Tool Cabinet

BY JAN ZOLTOWSKI

After a career of 35 years I had collected a substantial number of woodworking tools and I finally decided that they deserved a proper home. I set out to create a cabinet capable of holding my tools in a relatively small but accessible area. The result is home to well over 300 tools, yet covers only about 12 sq. ft. of wall.

I deliberately dedicated this cabinet to hand tools to keep them apart from dusty power tools, but the design can be modified easily to accommodate small power tools as well. Think twice before making the cabinet smaller; even if your tool collection would look lost in a cabinet of this size, it's nice to have space to grow into.

No Wasted Space

The inside surfaces of the main doors hold thin tools such as chisels and screwdrivers. Inside the cabinet, working down from the top, the upper shelf seats larger handplanes; the middle section has a pair of internal doors that support tools on both sides (increasing the hanging area by 40 percent) and that open to reveal additional space for saws and marking tools. The lower area is divided into cubbyholes for smoothing planes and other specialty planes, whereas six small drawers in the bottom hold smaller

tools such as block planes, drill bits, and router bits.

The cabinet hangs on upper and lower pairs of French cleats. Behind the cabinet, in the space between the cleats, is a place to hold a carpenter's square on one side, and three panel saws, held securely by means of the friction of their teeth, on the other. The cabinet holds all these tools within easy reach, and every blade and tooth stays sharp and protected.

Construction Starts with a Single Box

I built my cabinet out of Baltic-birch plywood. Not only is it more economical than solid lumber, but it eliminates problems such as stuck drawers from dimensional changes caused by the high humidity in the Northwest. The body of the cabinet starts out as one large box with the sides made from ¾-in.-thick plywood. Join the corners with ½-in. finger or box joints.

Rout a ½-in.-deep by ⅜-in.-wide rabbet around the inside front and back edges to accept panels of ½-in.-thick plywood. The front of the cabinet is attached with glue and nails, but the back is attached with screws only to allow access during later construction.

DRAWERS FOR SMALL OBJECTS. The six drawers at the bottom of the cabinet hold small objects such as block planes.

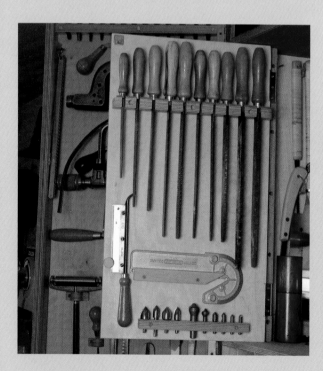

HINGED PANELS ADD STORAGE. Tools hang on both sides, adding 40 percent to the cabinet's hanging area.

STORAGE BEHIND THE CABINET. A carpenter's square on one side and three panel saws on the other fit into slots in the back of the cabinet.

Next, cut off approximately the front third of the box to form what will become the main doors. On the tablesaw, using the rip fence as a guide, cut through both ends of the box. Attach a thin piece of scrap plywood to each end by nailing it on both sides of the cut. This is to keep the two parts of the box attached while cutting through the long sides on the tablesaw.

While at the saw, cut the newly removed front section of the cabinet in half to form the two main doors. When this is done, attach pieces of ¾-in.-thick plywood to form the center side of each door. Don't worry about the exposed edges of the plywood sides; these will be covered by banding.

Create the Gallery and Drawers

The central gallery, with its cubbyholes used to store planes, gives the cabinet rigidity. Cut the upper and lower crosspieces, then cut the dadoes for the ¼-in.-thick shelf partitions either on the tablesaw or with a router. Use the same method to create the dado on the underside of the gallery to receive the center drawer divider.

A COMPACT CABINET WITH AMPLE CAPACITY

The cabinet is made almost entirely from birch plywood, which gives dimensional stability at a budget price. The main carcase is ¾-in.-thick plywood connected with finger joints.

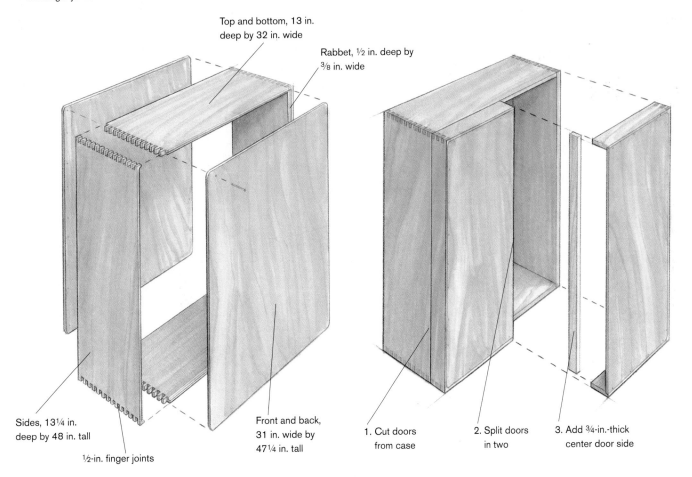

Top and bottom, 13 in. deep by 32 in. wide

Rabbet, ½ in. deep by ⅜ in. wide

Sides, 13¼ in. deep by 48 in. tall

½-in. finger joints

Front and back, 31 in. wide by 47¼ in. tall

1. Cut doors from case

2. Split doors in two

3. Add ¾-in.-thick center door side

Construct the Carcase

BUILD A BIG BOX. **The main body of the cabinet is connected at each corner with 1/2-in. finger joints cut on the tablesaw (below). Rabbet the front and rear for the panels. Glue and nail the front panel (right), but attach the rear with screws for interior access.**

CUT AWAY THE DOOR SECTION. **With the front and rear panels installed, cut away the front quarter of the box to form the main doors. Cut the short sides first, and then tack a batten across the cut to hold the section in place while cutting the long sides.**

NEXT CUT MAKES THE TWO MAIN DOORS. Tack two strips of wood
across the cut line as shown. Then set the sawblade to just score the
underside of the strips. In this way the panel is cut in half but won't
bind on the sawblade.

Before installing the gallery you need to make the drawers, because their height and spacing will determine the location of the gallery. The six drawers are made of ½-in.-thick plywood with ¼-in. finger joints. The bottoms, made of ¼-in.-thick plywood, sit in a rabbet rather than a groove because the latter would reduce the depth of these already-shallow drawers.

After unscrewing the back panel of the cabinet, rout a dado on each side for the upper shelf, and then glue in the shelf. Stack the drawers using laminate or thin cardboard as spacers, and mark the top of the stack for the location of the bottom dado of the gallery. Lay the gallery across the cabinet and mark the location of the top dado. Cut the pair of dadoes on each side, and then install the gallery and the central drawer divider. The latter is screwed to the bottom of the cabinet from the outside and is not dadoed, so as not to weaken the bottom of the cabinet.

I hung the drawers by attaching ¼-in.-thick by ½-in.-wide strips of hard maple to the sides of the cabinet and the central divider. To get the drawers to hang perfectly parallel, I used the same spacers when cutting rabbets in the drawer sides and when attaching the strips to the cabinet.

On a router table, create a guide channel the same width as the drawer sides comprising two outer guide strips, two center strips of wood the width of the straight-cut router bit, and two equal spacers to go above and below the bit that center the drawer side over the router bit. Clamp the outer strips to the table, remove the spacers and the center strips, raise the bit to ¼ in., and cut a groove until just before the finger joints at the front of the drawer.

When all the grooves have been cut, use the spacer strips from the router table and the laminate spacers used earlier when stacking the drawers to establish the location for each maple drawer runner.

Screw the runners to the sides, and the central divider and the drawers are hung.

The two inner doors and their posts are made from ⅝-in.-thick plywood. Cut matching recesses on each door and post for a pair of hinges, and then screw each post to the sides of the cabinet between the top of the torsion box and the upper shelf. Hang the doors on these posts.

The separate unit at the back of the cabinet is built of two layers of ¼-in.-thick plywood and should be designed to accommodate carpenter's squares and panel saws. Screw this unit to the back of the cabinet between the French cleats.

The outer doors are hung using piano hinges and magnetic catches; ball catches give a positive latch to the doors. After hanging the front doors, conceal the exposed rabbet joint around the front panel with a ³⁄₁₆-in.-thick by ¾-in.-wide strip of solid maple, rounded slightly (as all exposed corners should be).

With the main cabinet construction complete, make and attach custom hangers for each tool using scraps of plywood.

I finished my cabinet with two coats of oil-based sealer that were sanded with P320-grit sandpaper. Then I wiped on a couple of coats of tung oil.

The cubbyholes and the bottoms of the drawers were covered with industrial rubber–backed floor covering, available from home centers. It comes in many colors and gives excellent protection to edge tools. The final step was to attach pulls to the drawers and doors, and stout handles to the outside of the cabinet. These are a great help when you and a friend lift the cabinet onto the wall-mounted part of the cleats. Install all of the tools and then start putting them to use.

JAN ZOLTOWSKI is a professional antique and art restorer who lives near Seattle, Washington.

SHELVES AND CUBBYHOLES PROVIDE TOOL STORAGE

The internal doors are ⁵⁄₈ in. thick, the shelves are either ⁵⁄₈ in. or ½ in. thick, and the front and back are ½-in.-thick panels. The drawers are made from ½-in.-thick material with ¼-in.-thick plywood used for the drawer bottoms and the gallery dividers.

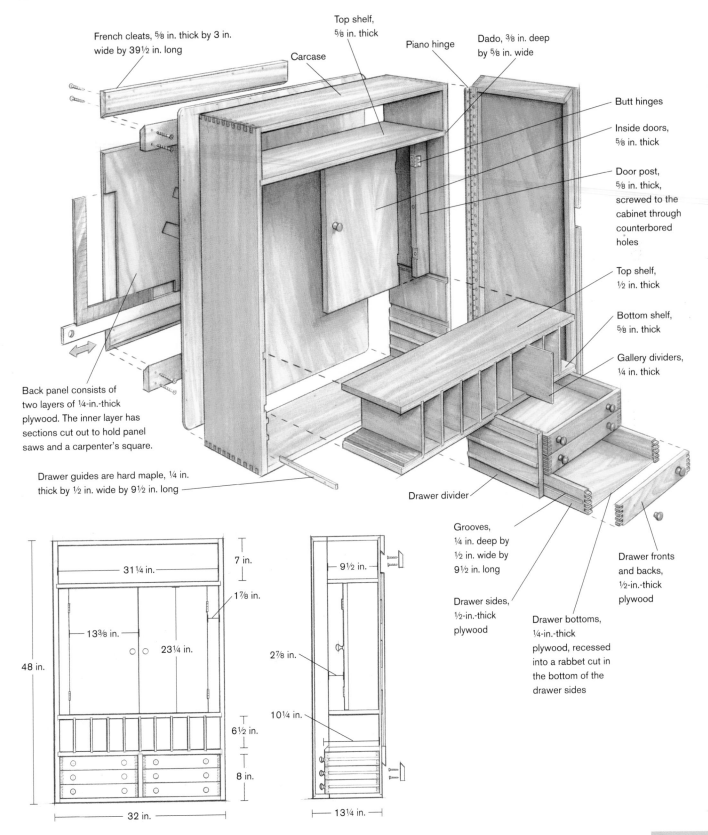

French cleats, ⁵⁄₈ in. thick by 3 in. wide by 39½ in. long

Top shelf, ⁵⁄₈ in. thick

Carcase

Piano hinge

Dado, ³⁄₈ in. deep by ⁵⁄₈ in. wide

Butt hinges

Inside doors, ⁵⁄₈ in. thick

Door post, ⁵⁄₈ in. thick, screwed to the cabinet through counterbored holes

Top shelf, ½ in. thick

Bottom shelf, ⁵⁄₈ in. thick

Gallery dividers, ¼ in. thick

Back panel consists of two layers of ¼-in.-thick plywood. The inner layer has sections cut out to hold panel saws and a carpenter's square.

Drawer guides are hard maple, ¼ in. thick by ½ in. wide by 9½ in. long

Drawer divider

Grooves, ¼ in. deep by ½ in. wide by 9½ in. long

Drawer sides, ½-in.-thick plywood

Drawer bottoms, ¼-in.-thick plywood, recessed into a rabbet cut in the bottom of the drawer sides

Drawer fronts and backs, ½-in.-thick plywood

7 in.

31¼ in.

1⅞ in.

13⅜ in.

23¼ in.

48 in.

9½ in.

2⅞ in.

10¼ in.

6½ in.

8 in.

32 in.

13¼ in.

Assemble the Interior

ATTACH THE INNER DOORS. Stretching from the top of the gallery to the bottom of the upper shelf, each inner door is hung from a post screwed to the cabinet.

INSTALL THE UPPER SHELF AND GALLERY. Cut a dado on both sides of the cabinet and install the upper shelf. This gives the carcase extra rigidity. After routing the dadoes for the upper and lower shelves, test-fit the gallery and then glue it in.

STORAGE BEHIND THE CABINET. An inner layer of 1/4-in.-thick plywood is cut to receive panel saws and a carpenter's square, then covered by a solid outer piece of plywood.

Basement Shop on Wheels

BY ANATOLE BURKIN

My first shop was an old garage nestled on a bank above Puget Sound near Seattle. It had an old plank floor with gaps wide enough to swallow small tools and hardware. For power I had one extension cord that snaked back to the house, and lighting was provided by an open garage door. I have fond memories of that shop, bundled up against the cold, working under natural light, hacking away and successfully cutting my first dovetail joint. I remind myself of those days when confronted by the limitations of my current shop, which by comparison is a dream.

My basement shop is only 20 ft. by 21 ft.—about the size of a two-car garage—but I've tackled projects as large as a run of kitchen cabinets. The secret to getting the most out of this small space is mobility. Almost everything rests on locking casters—machines, tables, and shop-built tool chests.

Storage and organization are also vital in a small space. The area under every machine tool or bench is utilized for storage. Yes, it does get crowded when I undertake a large project. But I can reconfigure the space as needed for milling, assembling, and finishing.

Layout for a Small Shop

Some tools are best left stationary. My tablesaw stays put because it's very bulky and heavy. And the dust collector must have a permanent home because of the metal ductwork attached to it. The rest of the shop was designed to work around these machines.

Machine tools, as well as benches, must be located where they can handle the largest piece of stock I am likely to use. And with a small dust collector, I have to keep duct runs to a minimum. I try to keep most of the mobile tools parked where they can be put into service easily.

In a small shop, you'll often see the tablesaw angled. This orientation takes advantage of the room's diagonal dimensions. That's a good solution, but it typically means the saw reaches into the center of the room. When I have a large project going, such as a run of cabinets, I like having the center of the shop available for assembly. I orient the tablesaw parallel and close to the shop's longest wall, which leaves me with more than enough room to cut a full sheet of plywood. The tablesaw's outfeed table is set on casters so that I can wheel it out of the way and use that space for spray finishing.

Convertible Shop

A small shop can't be all things at all times. Design it with adaptability in mind.

1. A roller, clamped to the bed of the jointer, which is placed close to the tablesaw, helps support wide stock for crosscutting.

2. To gain space in the center of the shop for assembly, the jointer may be moved.

3. The outfeed table wheels away to create a finishing area.

4. In preparation for spraying, a drop cloth is tossed over machines.

5. A wooden duct extension fits between the shopmade air cleaner and window frame to exhaust overspray.

6. The fine-particle filter has been replaced with a coarse furnace filter to capture finish before it blows outdoors.

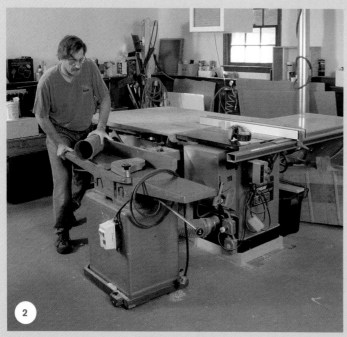

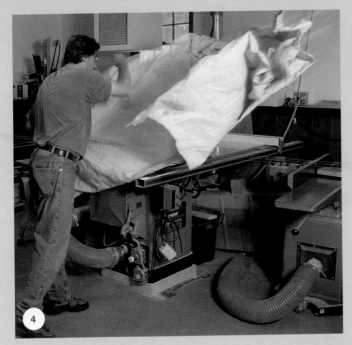

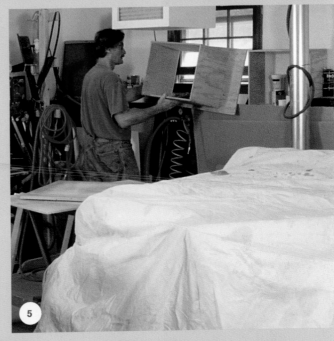

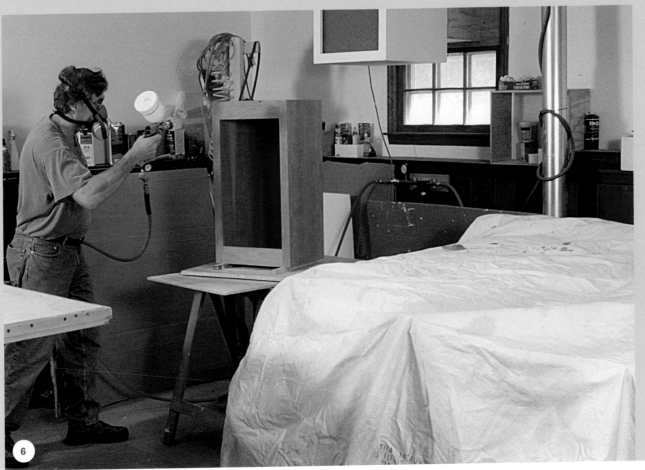

In a crowded space, adjoining tools can be set up to work with, not hinder, one another.

In a crowded space, adjoining tools can be set up to work with, not hinder, one another. Although I'd like to have a sliding table for my tablesaw, I haven't the space. But I use my 8-in. jointer, which is parked to the left of the saw, to assist with sheet goods. At a scrap metal yard I picked up a set of metal rollers from a conveyor assembly. I made a wooden frame for the roller that allows it to be clamped to the jointer bed and provides support when handling sheet goods. Total outlay was about $2.

The jointer-tablesaw pairing didn't work at first because the jointer fence was higher than the tabletop of the saw. Lowering the jointer seemed like a lot of work, so I raised the tablesaw on blocks. It turns out that the added height has made repetitive tasks, such as tenoning, much more comfortable for my 6-ft. frame.

Plenty of Room for the Chopsaw

Although the chopsaw is small, it's called upon to handle very long stock. Finding the perfect spot was a compromise. There isn't room for a dedicated chopsaw stand with 8-ft.-long wings on both sides, so I use my European-style workbench to serve as one wing. A piece of scrap laid across the table serves as a low-tech outfeed support. To the left of the chopsaw, I use another one of those scrap-yard conveyor rollers to make it easy to slide stock into place.

Chopsaws spray sawdust all over the place, and while I haven't totally solved the problem, my method works okay. The key component is a capture box behind the saw to catch dust that's kicked back. A 5-in. port is added to the top of the box and connects to my dust-collection system. Additionally, I run a small hose from the saw's dust port (where the bag goes) and snake it a few inches into the 5-in. dust-collector hose. Whatever doesn't go up the hoses eventually settles into the capture box.

Thicknessing Machines

I have more thicknessing machines than I really have a right to own, but I've figured out a way to keep them from being a nuisance. For taking a thin pass or thicknessing highly figured woods, nothing beats a portable thickness planer with rubber infeed and outfeed rollers. Bigger machines, such as my 15-in. thickness planer, are good for hogging off material, not delicate passes. And when it comes to removing tearout from highly figured woods or sanding shopmade veneer, I appreciate every penny I spent on my drum-style thickness sander.

MACHINES TO SURFACE STOCK. The 15-in. planer can remove stock quickly. The bench-top planer riding piggyback excels at taking light passes without leaving knife marks. And a drum sander (not shown) speeds up what most consider the least enjoyable part of woodworking.

Because I only use one of these tools at a time, I have one dust hose hanging from the ceiling to serve them all. To save space, I mounted the small planer piggyback on the larger one. Although the portable unit can be lifted off and placed on a bench, I typically just leave it in place and plane boards at chest height. Below the planer and sander I've installed shelving to store sanding belts and other tools.

A Simple, Functional Router Table

My router table has evolved over the years. It now features dust collection above and below, bit storage, and a top large enough to hold a second router.

A large reducer (10 in. to 5 in.) is set into the base of the cabinet and connects to the dust collector. On top, the fence has a port for a 2½-in.-dia. hose. A pair of doors allows easy access to the router. The cabinet is set on wheels so that it can be moved to a corner when not in use.

Places to Store Tools

I have a small, simple tool rack near my workbench in which I keep chisels, handsaws, mallets, and hammers. The workbench has two shelves to store all of the hand-

SAWDUST IS CAPTURED BY A BOX, WHICH IS CONNECTED TO THE DUST COLLECTOR. A roller bolted to the left of the table provides stock support. The workbench (with the aid of a piece of scrap) provides support to the right of the chopsaw.

TRAVELING ROUTER CABINET. Dust collection is provided below, via a 10 in. to 5 in. reducer, and above, via a 2½-in.-dia. hose connected to the fence. The table is big enough to add another router if needed.

Storage and organization are vital in a small space. The area under every machine tool or bench is utilized for storage.

planes I own. Now that the shelves are full, I know I have enough of them.

Most other small tools are kept in mobile shop-built carts. One houses everything I own for drilling and screwing. Most of the time it sits next to the drill press, but when I'm assembling parts, I roll the cart to where I'm working. The other cart contains measuring tools as well as all-around stuff, such as mechanic's wrenches and drivers. Both carts can also serve as stock carriers, for moving parts from one machine to another. (The mobile router table can also be used this way.)

The idea of putting all of my clamps in a trash can isn't new. But to keep the long pipe clamps from tipping over the can,

I built a simple rack that is screwed into the can and keeps the clamps more or less upright. The can is mounted on a dolly, so I can move it around.

Low-Cost Electrics and Pneumatics

I originally lit my shop using cheap shop-light fixtures that cost about $7 apiece, and that worked out to about a buck a year before they began failing. I recently swapped them with flush-mount fixtures of a higher quality that have electronic ballasts, which are quieter and turn on instantly. The fixtures also use T-8 bulbs, which are more energy efficient. I connected them using a plastic track system that is quite compact and easy to install. Most home centers sell these fixtures, and it's an inexpensive way for a nonelectrician to set up a very satisfactory lighting system. I spent about $250 for the five fixtures and hardware.

The shop did not have 240-volt power when I moved in. To keep down costs, I went with PVC conduit, installed on the rear outside wall of the house. Then I routed enough wire through the conduit to give me a gang of three 240-volt circuits. A 12-gauge extension cord, snaked along the main dust-collection duct, brings 240-volt power to the middle of the shop.

I find a lot of uses for compressed air: everything from pneumatic tools to clearing out dust from wood pores before spray finishing. I didn't want to go to the trouble of plumbing my shop, but at the same time I didn't want just one large coil of hose to drag from one part of the shop to the other. The solution is a three-in-one manifold and filter that allows me to provide clean, dry air to three locations both inexpensively and quickly. One long hose runs out to the garage. Another long one snakes along the ductwork and provides air to the opposite side of the shop. Near the compressor, a short run of hose provides air for spray finishing.

Spray Finishing without a Booth

I like to spray finish. You can't beat a spray gun for speed and the amount of control it brings to the task. But I don't have room for a spray booth. Nonetheless, I can spray in the shop without worrying about dust specks by using a two-pronged approach. First, I clean the shop before finishing. I'm not overly fussy about the cleanup except in the corner where I spray. Second, I use fast-drying finishes, such as water-based products or shellac. I don't spray slow-drying or highly flammable finishes.

Spray finishing also requires a method of removing the overspray. I installed a large industrial fan in a box made of medium-density fiberboard and hung it in front of a window. When I spray, I open the window and press-fit an extension duct to the fan box, which helps direct the air outdoors without fouling the window casing. The fan box has a slot for a coarse furnace filter in front, which catches much of the finish before it reaches the fan. Without the extension duct in place, the fan doubles as an air cleaner. For that application, I use a fine-particle filter. (In warm weather, one could just flush the air outdoors.)

The tablesaw outfeed table doubles as my spray-finish bench for small objects. To keep it and the saw clean, I cover the entire setup with a large drop cloth. For larger pieces, I unclamp the outfeed table from the saw and roll it out of the way. And to keep finish off the walls and floor, I keep on hand large pieces of cardboard, such as those used to package appliances.

A Shop is Never Done

I've been itching to get my hands on an old lathe but haven't found one yet. In the meantime, I've rearranged the shop in my head a number of times to make room for a newcomer. Try as I might, I'm not sure I can fit one more large tool in that space.

Which leaves me thinking that maybe it's time to consider a freestanding building or moving to another location with the sort of shop space everyone craves: a large barn with a loft. I could get a few hundred bucks selling all of the used casters, enough to buy a nice, new handplane. But until then, I'll enjoy the space I have.

ANATOLE BURKIN is the publisher of *Fine Woodworking* and an avid woodworker.

CLAMPS TO GO. Stored in a metal trash can, clamps can be wheeled to the assembly area, then rolled into an out-of-the way corner when not needed.

Not Your Father's Pegboard

BY HANK GILPIN

The first thing people notice when they visit my shop is the tool rack. Not the wood scattered and stacked everywhere, not the furniture under construction, not the big old machines. Nope, they always walk over to the wall of open tool and clamp storage and say, "Wow, your shop is so organized."

I'm never sure if the shop's neatness is a letdown or a pleasant surprise. But it doesn't really matter. I didn't build my tool rack for display. I am neat by nature and by need fairly organized. We do a lot of handwork at my shop, and because I always have at least one other person working with me, I wanted a rack that would put the full array of hand tools within arm's length of two benches.

The wall's layout is simple and practical. Each of the primary tools—every plane, chisel, file, measuring device, and saw—has a spot to sit in and can be taken out without moving anything else. Blades stay sharp, squares stay true, and saws stay straight. The slanted shelves for the planes and chisels make the tools easy to locate and grab. A strip of wood tacked along the lower edge of these shelves keeps the tools from sliding off, and $5/16$-in.-sq. strips between the tools keep them spaced properly.

The shallow shelves above the plane and chisel racks hold sanding blocks, mallets, drills, and the less frequently used planes and scrapers. At the bottom of the rack is hanging storage for clamps and shelving for the myriad blocks, wedges, battens, and pads used with the clamps.

I didn't rush into the rack's design. I thought about my work habits and sketched out a number of alternative arrangements. But I built the entire project in one day. I used construction-grade plywood and nailed and glued it together. I don't think I could come up with a simpler, easier-to-use solution. After 24 years of use, it serves the shop well.

HANK GILPIN has been designing and building fine art furniture for almost 30 years.

ORGANIZATION OUT IN THE OPEN. It's easier to stay organized when tool storage is close at hand and unobstructed. The convenience of the author's simple system keeps tools from piling up on the bench.

Three Ways to Rack Lumber

BY MATTHEW TEAGUE

Storing Sheet Goods

For John West, a cabinetmaker in Danbury, Conn., storing a large amount of sheet goods is an inevitable part of the job. "The general-use stuff we keep vertically," he says. "If it's something that'll be here a while, we store it horizontally."

West's racks are held off the ground with 2x3 lumber (he uses three boards sandwiched and bolted together) and plywood. Vertical bays are 18 in. wide and 12 ft. deep. Four horizontal racks are built one over the other and used to store sheet goods flat. The horizontal racks are 6 ft. wide, constructed out of 2x6s, and have a plywood top. All the racks are held together with bolts.

"It is important to build something that will be big enough to handle anything you might have," says West. "Fiberboard comes about 5 ft. 1 in. wide in 10 ft. and 12 ft. lengths. The racks are 5 ft. 3 in. on the same principle. It would be easy to build a smaller rack for whatever you might need."

STAYING FLEXIBLE. John West designed his system based on the heavy supply of sheet goods his projects often entail, but the stalls accommodate varying types of stock as his needs change.

No Frills Storage

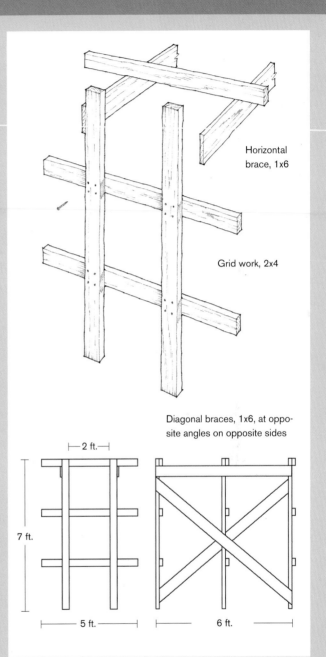

Kelly Mehler, a woodworker and teacher living in Berea, Ky., uses lumber racks that are as simple and efficient as you'll find. It doesn't take days or even hours to build a similar setup. "It looks like a tic-tac-toe board standing straight up," he says. "You'd be amazed how much strength you get out of a 2x4 when it's standing on its end." He's built three of these 2x4 grids. They stand straight up and are connected with horizontal 1x6 lumber. Each rack has nine holes with openings that are about 2 ft. sq., and the boards just slide right in.

"The flow of work is very important to me," Mehler says. He has two racks built this way—one on either side of his radial-arm saw. "I just pull the boards right off the racks and onto the radial-arm saw and rough mill them to size."

"It's all just nailed together," he says. "Screws would be better, but I didn't really think about it when I put them up 18 years ago."

Horizontal brace, 1x6

Grid work, 2x4

Diagonal braces, 1x6, at opposite angles on opposite sides

2 ft.

7 ft.

5 ft.

6 ft.

BUILT TO LAST. Kelly Mehler has used the same basic rack for more than 18 years. He stacks boards in the order they came off the tree and often lets them dry for a year or more.

Finding an orderly way to store lumber is integral to creating an efficient shop. Side-stepping boards to get to machines and benches is not only unsafe, it's also no way to spend a day. For most, the key to a good storage system is keeping lumber out of the way but close at hand in as small an area as possible. There are almost as many storage methods as there are woodworkers. A look at three different lumber racks might help you adopt the system that will work best in your own shop.

MATTHEW TEAGUE is a furniture maker and writer based in Nashville, Tennessee.

Going Vertical

After 19 years as a stairbuilder, teacher, and spare-time kayak builder in Long Beach, Calif., Lon Schleining prefers vertical storage. "As a matter of fact," he says, "I moved into my shop because it had a high ceiling." Schleining says that vertical storage saves him valuable time and labor. "My old shop had a low ceiling, and it seemed like the board I was after was always at the bottom of the pile. All I did was stack and unstack and move lumber around. It was like a gift from God when I got to a space where I could get to any board rapidly."

The boards are stored on end on a platform and are held up vertically by angled 2x4s. "I really stole the design from a local hardware store," he says. "They have big A-frames with lumber stored on both sides. I just built half of that and bolted it to the wall."

He also uses 1x6 plywood indexers that are notched to move on a horizontal board to denote and separate different species. "It makes it ever so handy," he says, "like having your paperwork in files."

A HANDY FILE OF WOODS. You won't find Lon Schleining spending his day stacking and unstacking boards. His vertical storage system uses plywood indexers to separate species and keeps everything in easy reach.

Lumber Storage Solutions

BY ANDY BEASLEY

I once read that the idea of infinite space was perhaps the most difficult concept for the mind of man to grasp. I beg to differ. Anyone who ever has tried to create a functional shop knows that fitting it into a finite space is a far more challenging proposition. Once all of the necessary tools, materials, and that last bottle of glue have been shoehorned into the workshop, you can find yourself on the outside looking in.

When building my shop several years ago, I experimented with different layouts until I found the one that worked best for me. I've been happy with the result, largely because the lumber-storage system I developed added considerably to the efficiency of my shop while taking up little of its finite space.

Wall Rack Handles the Long Stuff

The centerpiece of my storage system is a horizontal rack along one wall. The rack is exceptionally stable, and the various levels hold a lot of material within a small footprint. The design is straightforward, the materials are relatively inexpensive, and the construction time is short.

I frequently store 16-ft. lengths of molding, so I decided to install six vertical

Wall Rack for Lumber

With stanchions spaced 32 in. on center, the rack can be made to fit a wall of any length and height.

LUMBER AT THE READY. A wall-mounted rack keeps lumber organized and accessible without taking up valuable floor space.

SIMPLE MOUNTING SYSTEM. Lumber rests on a series of support arms that are bolted to stanchions.

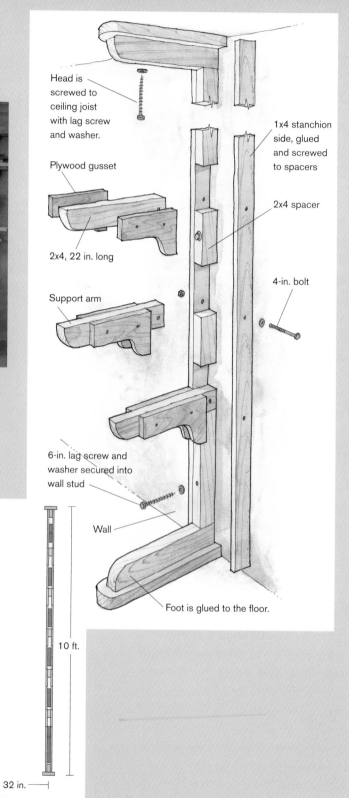

Head is screwed to ceiling joist with lag screw and washer.

Plywood gusset

2x4, 22 in. long

Support arm

1x4 stanchion side, glued and screwed to spacers

2x4 spacer

4-in. bolt

6-in. lag screw and washer secured into wall stud

Wall

Foot is glued to the floor.

10 ft.

32 in.

stanchions to provide the necessary horizontal space. The 2x6 studs in the shop wall are on 16-in. centers; I installed a stanchion on every other one, or 32 in. on center. These stanchions are merely lengths of 1x4 pine, glued and nailed to 2x4 spacers. The spacers add stiffness, create pockets for the support arms, and provide a solid attachment point for the lag screws that mount the assembly to the wall.

Although the stanchion assembly is simple to build, it helps to choose stock that is straight, without bow or twist. Gluing and nailing the pieces together on a level floor is an easy way to keep them true.

This rack is designed to support considerable weight if it is mounted securely to a sturdy wall. To attach the stanchions to the shop wall, I first marked the locations of the electrical wires in the wall so that I could give them a wide berth. Then I secured the stanchions with 6-in. lag screws through the spacer blocks and into the wall studs.

This rack can be attached equally well to a concrete wall as long as heavy-duty masonry anchors are used. The small, plastic expanding anchors used to hang pictures on cinderblock walls won't provide the necessary pull-out resistance. For similar reasons, don't mount this rack to a hollow gypsum or paneled wall.

The head and foot of each stanchion help prevent twisting, stabilizing the rack when it's under load. The head is screwed to a ceiling truss, while the matching foot is glued securely to the floor.

The horizontal support arms do the hard work. They're made of 2x4s with ¾-in.-thick plywood gussets screwed to each side. I angled the arms upward 2 degrees to keep material from sliding off, and I rounded the protruding ends to soften any inadvertent collision between my head and one of the arms. My wife painted most of the rack before installation. However, to prevent lumber from picking

Cart for Lumber Offcuts

Simplified frame-and-panel construction means the cart assembles without much fuss, yet has plenty of strength.

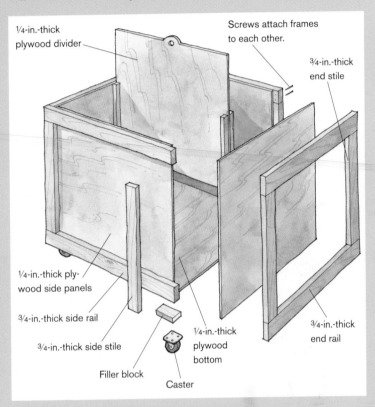

¼-in.-thick plywood divider

Screws attach frames to each other.

¾-in.-thick end stile

¼-in.-thick plywood side panels

¾-in.-thick side rail

¾-in.-thick side stile

Filler block

Caster

¼-in.-thick plywood bottom

¾-in.-thick end rail

ROLLING CART ADDS CONVENIENCE. A framed plywood box on wheels provides the perfect place to store offcuts.

up unwanted stains, the top edge of each arm was left unpainted.

I started at the top row and installed each arm by drilling a hole through the stanchions and the inner end of the arm. A ½-in.-dia., 4-in.-long bolt secures each arm. In the future, though, should I decide to change the elevation of the arms, the oversize pockets in the stanchions give me the ability to drill a new bolt hole and shift each arm to a new location.

Roll-Around Cart for Short Pieces

Besides death, taxes, and slivers, I think the accumulation of lumber offcuts is about the only thing woodworkers can take for granted. The woodstove can handle just so much, and besides, that peanut-size chunk of walnut may come in handy someday. Owning up to my pack-rat tendencies, I built three storage carts for offcuts that fit in the unused area under the bottom shelf of the wall rack. I left the rest of that area open for future storage needs.

The carts are simple boxes on casters. To stave off the chaos that would ensue if I just threw scrap into the carts, I installed removable dividers, which allow for a rough sort of organization. By adding a removable plywood top to one of the carts, I immediately had a mobile workbench.

Vertical Box Stores Sheet Goods in Minimal Space

I'd initially planned to store sheet goods flat or on some sort of horizontal cart, but I discarded those ideas because they ate up too much floor space. The obvious answer was vertical storage. Holding 15 to 20 sheets, the rack I constructed is little more than a doubled-up plywood bottom, a few 2x4 posts, and a plywood top.

Because there's little outward pressure on this type of rack, it can be attached to a wall with either nails or wood screws. To this simple structure, I added a few user-friendly features. The 2x4 spacers on the side walls of the rack give me some finger room when I want to withdraw a sheet that's located near the edge. A layer of Plexiglas covering the plywood bottom makes sliding even the heaviest sheet a breeze. And because I don't relish the idea of dinging the corner of an expensive sheet, I installed a pull-out pad to protect the pivoting corner as I load or unload material. To squeeze the last bit of utility from the rack, I use the outer frame as a place to hang levels, squares, and cutting jigs.

A Storage System Works Only if You Use It

Just as a closet won't pick up that shirt you've thrown over a chair, a lumber rack won't do you any good if you don't use it. I've developed habits to keep the shop both uncluttered and efficient. At the end of each day, I select the offcuts I intend to keep. Any boards shorter than 24 in. go into the roll-around lumber cart; longer pieces are stored on the horizontal rack. I used to put these leftovers anywhere, but each time I brought in a new load of boards, I had too many little things to rearrange before I could place the incoming material on the rack.

When I return plywood or sheet goods to the vertical rack, I always write the new width on the exposed edge. That prevents miscalculations when I'm reviewing the material I have on hand for a project, and I don't have to slide out a piece to check its width.

This storage system works exceptionally well. Now, when work is going smoothly and all my materials are stowed neatly away, I sometimes let my mind wander to those minor problems of infinity.

ANDY BEASLEY is a woodworker and writer who lives with his wife, Peg, in the mountains of Colorado.

Rack for Sheet Goods

Stored vertically in this rack, sheet goods like plywood and medium-density fiberboard can be accessed with relative ease.

CHOOSE AND USE. This vertical rack makes it easy to flip through the sheets and pull one out without damaging it.

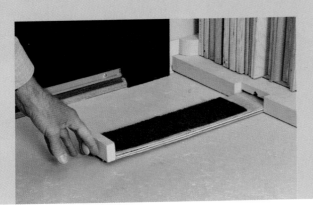

PROTECTIVE PAD. The outside bottom corners of sheet goods get some protection from damage, thanks to a pull-out pad.

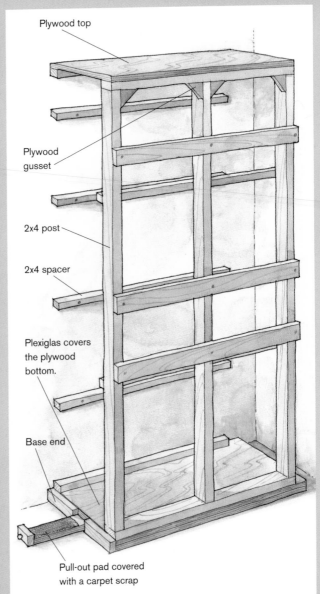

Plywood top

Plywood gusset

2x4 post

2x4 spacer

Plexiglas covers the plywood bottom.

Base end

Pull-out pad covered with a carpet scrap

Fine-Tune
Your Shop

BY JERRY H. LYONS

Assembly Cart Raises Work

This shopmade cart provides a comfortable working height (about 24 in.) and easy access to the back and sides of a large project, like this slant-top secretary (right). Also, the cart makes it easier and safer to roll a piece around my shop to take advantage of natural light. Both shelves are carpeted to protect the edges of the workpiece, and the lower shelf provides storage for components and hardware.

A SECRETARY ON THE MOVE. This rolling cart allows Lyons to move work around the shop easily. It also keeps a piece at a comfortable working height, with access to all sides.

I had long dreamed of creating a perfect shop and using it to teach woodworking. I reached that goal five years ago when I purchased a 3,000-sq.-ft. ranch-style log cabin near my home. I converted that space into a shop where I do woodwork and offer classes on the subject.

Two words describe my workshop environment: clean and organized. As long as I can remember, I have needed a place for everything and everything in its place. I may have inherited the trait in school woodshop as the student who cleaned up after every class. Or perhaps my most recent career as a training and safety consultant,

declaring the benefits of organization and systemization, has rubbed off on me.

Working in such a large space, I needed to keep hand tools organized, so I designed wall-mounted storage panels that make it easy to see and access tools. To make the workspace more efficient and adaptable, I also employ a variety of worktables and rolling carts, which do double duty as storage for project parts, related hardware, and even hand tools and jigs.

JERRY H. LYONS, who taught furniture making for 21 years, recently built his dream shop near Glasgow, Kentucky.

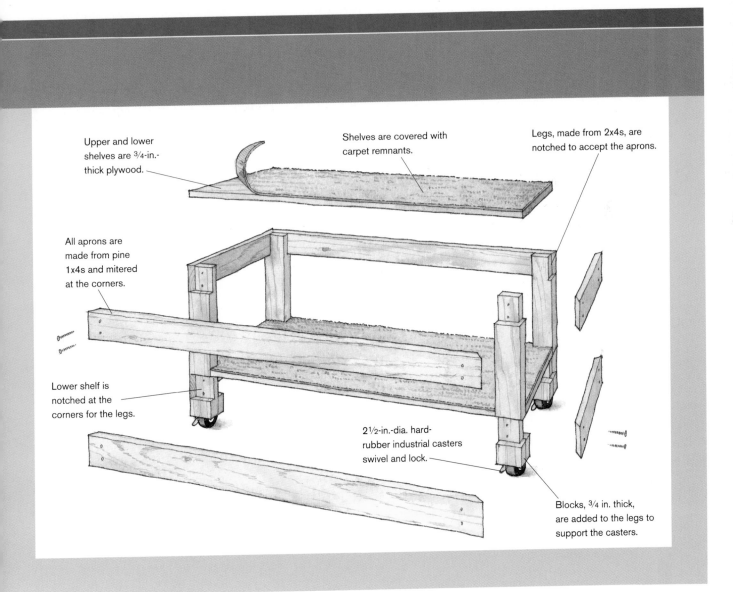

Upper and lower shelves are 3/4-in.-thick plywood.

Shelves are covered with carpet remnants.

Legs, made from 2x4s, are notched to accept the aprons.

All aprons are made from pine 1x4s and mitered at the corners.

Lower shelf is notched at the corners for the legs.

2 1/2-in.-dia. hard-rubber industrial casters swivel and lock.

Blocks, 3/4 in. thick, are added to the legs to support the casters.

Wall Panels Organize Hand Tools

Like many woodworkers, I have lots of hand tools, and I want to be able to find a tool when I need it. I would rather spend my time working than looking. To organize my hand-tool collection, I built four tool panels near my workbenches. Each tool, regardless of its size, fits into its own space within one of these panels. The panel backs are made of ¾-in.-thick seven-ply oak plywood. The edging is solid oak rabbeted to receive the plywood and mitered at the corners.

To accommodate the needs of several students at once, all panels include common tools such as handsaws and planes. Whenever possible, I grouped tools—such as those for measuring, layout, and cutting—according to use.

I used a bandsaw, handplanes, and sanders to shape and mold each tool holder's unique configuration. I glued the tool holders in place and used screws and dowels for reinforcement.

DESIGNS ON DISPLAY. Lyons finds it helpful to keep plans for his current project displayed so that he can reference them easily but not get them damaged.

TOOLS ARE GROUPED ACCORDING TO USE. Layout tools and clamps are gathered on this tool panel.

A PLACE FOR EVERYTHING. Wall panels display hand tools, making them easy to find and access.

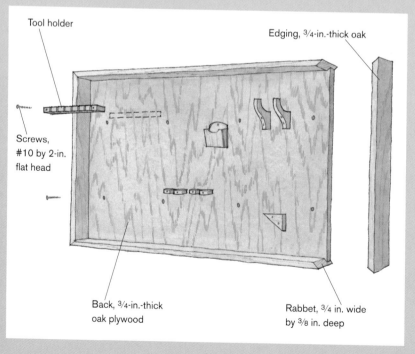

Tool holder

Edging, ¾-in.-thick oak

Screws, #10 by 2-in. flat head

Back, ¾-in.-thick oak plywood

Rabbet, ¾ in. wide by ⅜ in. deep

Clamping Table Tackles Glue-Ups

Gluing boards into panels often calls for at least three pairs of hands: one to keep the boards aligned, one to stop the clamps from falling over, and one to clean up the surplus glue. I solved this problem by making a dedicated clamping table.

The front and back edgings of the table are slotted to position I-beam bar clamps in an upright position. The tray below is covered with newspapers to catch glue squeeze-out. When done, I simply fold up the newspapers and discard them. This table also has a lower shelf to hold extra newspapers, several jigs, and occasionally used items.

I used a variety of scraps of plywood and solid stock to build the table, then I painted the whole piece with left-over floor paint. This has the bonus of making glue cleanup easier. Size the table based on what scraps are available and the kind of work you do. My table is 30½ in. deep by 65 in. wide by 32 in. tall.

LESS STRESS AND LESS MESS. The slotted table frame holds clamps in position while gluing up boards. Any glue squeeze-out drips into the newspaper-lined tray.

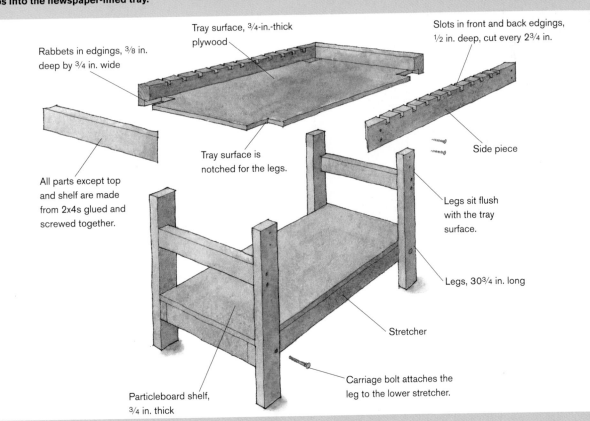

Rabbets in edgings, ⅜ in. deep by ¾ in. wide

Tray surface, ¾-in.-thick plywood

Slots in front and back edgings, ½ in. deep, cut every 2¾ in.

All parts except top and shelf are made from 2x4s glued and screwed together.

Tray surface is notched for the legs.

Side piece

Legs sit flush with the tray surface.

Legs, 30¾ in. long

Stretcher

Carriage bolt attaches the leg to the lower stretcher.

Particleboard shelf, ¾ in. thick

Mobile Table Serves Many Needs

This table is my heavyweight shop assistant: With a 1,000-lb. capacity, it never complains of backache; four wheels means it can move anywhere on the heavy-machinery floor; and because its wheels lock, the table never backs out when I need it most. The table is ⅛ in. below the height of the tablesaw to eliminate boards getting caught on it when being ripped. It can be positioned either lengthwise or widthwise, depending on the shape of the board being cut. It also makes a nice outfeed surface when planing long parts. In addition, it is a handy table for layout work as well as a good place to store clamps and other accessories. As with the clamping table, the dimensions of your table will differ based on your tools and the work you do.

A MULTIPURPOSE SUPPORT TABLE. This table can be wheeled to support operations at the tablesaw or the jointer, while the base stores clamps and jigs.

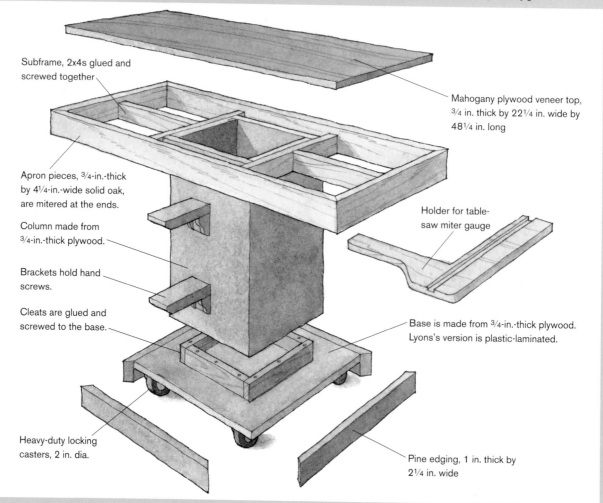

Subframe, 2x4s glued and screwed together

Mahogany plywood veneer top, ¾ in. thick by 22¼ in. wide by 48¼ in. long

Apron pieces, ¾-in.-thick by 4¼-in.-wide solid oak, are mitered at the ends.

Column made from ¾-in.-thick plywood.

Brackets hold hand screws.

Holder for table-saw miter gauge

Cleats are glued and screwed to the base.

Base is made from ¾-in.-thick plywood. Lyons's version is plastic-laminated.

Heavy-duty locking casters, 2 in. dia.

Pine edging, 1 in. thick by 2¼ in. wide

Roll-Away Workshop

BY BILL ENDRESS

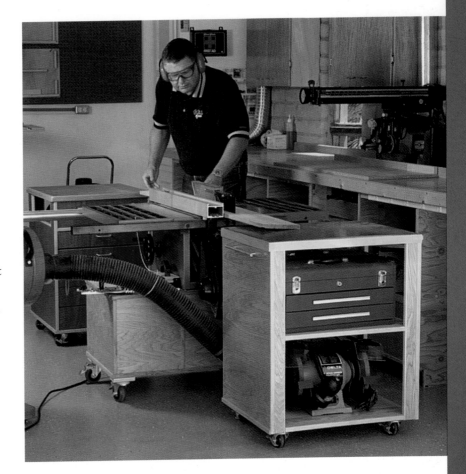

After many years living in central Florida, I received an invitation to relocate to Tucson, Ariz. Having been an active woodworker for 18 years, I placed adequate shop space high on my list when it came time to buy a home. Although it would have been nice to find a house with a separate workshop, my wife and I settled on one with a spacious 23-ft. by 23-ft. two-car garage.

This presented me with a challenge: create an efficient and comfortable workshop that could accommodate big projects but still make room for the family cars. So I began laying out the basic requirements needed to share my tablesaw with my parking space.

The primary requirement was to keep at least one car in the garage at night, even if a half-finished project occupied floor space. The flexibility to park two vehicles in the garage on occasion also was essential. The challenge was balancing these requirements with the elements of a good shop: one that is attractive to work in, easy to clean, and has plenty of organized storage. My philosophy throughout was "a place for everything, and everything in its place."

TWO CARS AND A WORKBENCH

The 23-ft.-sq. space is a workshop by day and a garage by night. A long workbench spanning one wall houses a series of multipurpose rolling cabinets used for storage and as tool stands, work surfaces, and infeed and outfeed tables.

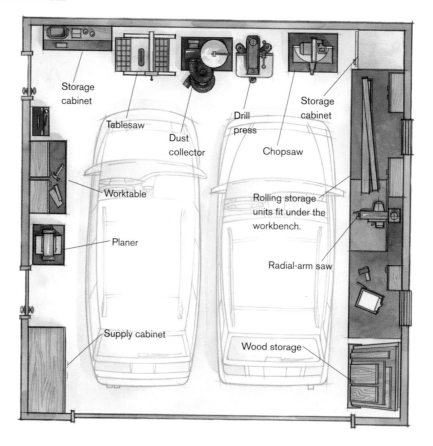

Storage cabinet

Tablesaw

Dust collector

Drill press

Storage cabinet

Chopsaw

Worktable

Rolling storage units fit under the workbench.

Planer

Radial-arm saw

Supply cabinet

Wood storage

Configure the Cabinet for Various Uses

Although confined to set dimensions, Endress designed the rolling cabinets with various arrangements of shelves and drawers so that each one serves a different purpose.

SLIDING SHELVES STORE POWER TOOLS VISIBLY AND WITHIN REACH. Rolling cabinets with various arrangements of shelves and drawers serve different purposes.

SHALLOW DRAWERS HOLD HAND TOOLS. An open area below the top of the cabinet keeps tools within reach but out of the way. The cabinet's top has enough overhang for attaching clamps.

THERE'S NO SUCH THING AS TOO MUCH STORAGE. Two tall, open shelves are used for storing large objects such as a toolbox, benchtop grinder, and belt sander.

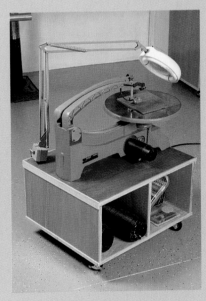

SCROLLSAW SITS AT A COMFORTABLE HEIGHT. The scrollsaw is mounted to this low rolling cabinet so that it can fit below the workbench when not in use. However, it's just the right height to use while sitting comfortably in a chair.

ROUTER TABLE HOLDS PARTS AND ACCESSORIES. This rolling router table is equipped with a router lift. The lift is offset to accommodate drawers, bits, and accessories. Dust-collection ports are built into the fence and cabinet back.

BASIC CONSTRUCTION OF ROLLING CABINETS

Each rolling cabinet has the same overall dimensions: 26 in. deep by 22 in. wide by 32½ in. high (the chopsaw, planer, and scrollsaw cabinets are shorter but follow a similar construction method). Locking swivel casters account for 3 in. of the height. The basic construction allows for variations in the placement of drawers and shelves. Each cabinet is constructed from ¾-in.-thick plywood and finished with two coats of water-based varnish.

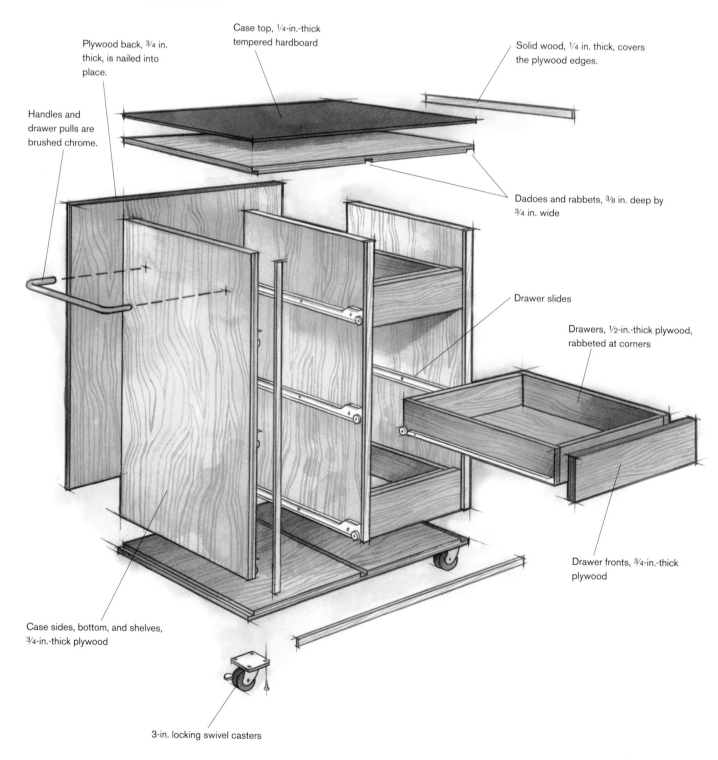

Plywood back, ¾ in. thick, is nailed into place.

Case top, ¼-in.-thick tempered hardboard

Solid wood, ¼ in. thick, covers the plywood edges.

Handles and drawer pulls are brushed chrome.

Dadoes and rabbets, ⅜ in. deep by ¾ in. wide

Drawer slides

Drawers, ½-in.-thick plywood, rabbeted at corners

Drawer fronts, ¾-in.-thick plywood

Case sides, bottom, and shelves, ¾-in.-thick plywood

3-in. locking swivel casters

Making Do with Limited Space

To have plenty of workspace and be able to cut long boards with my radial-arm saw, I knew I would build a long workbench along one of the garage walls. I began sketching idea after idea, looking for inspiration in books, magazines, and on TV woodworking shows.

While paging through magazines, I came upon an article for a roll-around tool-storage cabinet designed to be tucked under one wing of a tablesaw. It dawned on me that I could use a similar concept to save space in my garage. Beneath the workbench I could house roll-around cabinets to store tools.

The more I thought about it, the more advantages I could see of this system. With the rolling cabinets built to well-planned heights, they could serve as infeed and outfeed supports for the tablesaw, planer, and miter saw. Work areas also could be adapted to accommodate different projects just by rearranging the rolling cabinets.

Workbench Serves as a Garage for Rolling Cabinets

Constructing the main workbench was the first task. Because of space limitations, I decided to build it in two sections and bolt them together. One section is 8 ft. long, and the other is 6 ft. long. After some measuring of tables and kitchen cabinets, I determined that a work surface 30 in. deep and 37 in. high would be most comfortable. The workbench was fortified with a 2x4 frame to support the substantial weight of the radial-arm saw. I also installed two electrical-outlet strips on the bench, one on each side of the saw. They're mounted along the front edge to keep power-tool cords from extending across the top of the work surface.

Cabinets Are Built for Mixing and Matching

It was both fun and challenging to design and build the cabinets. Once I knew the workbench measurements, it was easy to back out the dimensions for the rolling cabinets. To keep it simple, the cabinets follow the same basic design but are configured differently, according to their functions.

Some cabinets have drawers, some have shelves, and some are built to hold large power tools. All of the cabinets roll on swivel casters. Handles are attached to the cabinet faces so that they can be maneuvered around the garage. The handles, drawer pulls, and cabinet-door handles are all matching brushed chrome, giving the final profile of the workbench a handsome look.

Storage cabinets double as work surfaces The cabinet used for storing power tools has six sliding shelves that pull out to the left for storing sanders, a jigsaw, and other tools. A second cabinet is built in a mirror image with shelves that pull out to the right. By butting these two cabinets together, a continuous work surface is created while leaving the shelves accessible.

A third rolling cabinet has five drawers to hold hand tools. A shelf underneath the top of the cabinet is open on three sides, providing a place to set tools and keep them out of the way. The opening also is useful for clamping workpieces to the tabletop, as clamp heads can be tightened against the top's overhang.

The fourth rolling cabinet simply has two shelves that are accessible from three sides. One shelf holds two toolboxes, and the other holds my bench grinder and a small belt sander.

The height of the cabinets is consistent and makes them ideal to serve as infeed and outfeed tables for my miter saw, planer, and tablesaw (see the photos on p. 127).

Stationary tools get wheels, too The first four cabinets provide adequate storage for my hand tools. But I also needed storage for my assortment of power tools.

The scrollsaw fits below the workbench, sitting on a low, rolling cabinet. Although it seems quite short at first glance, the cabinet is just the right height to use the saw while sitting comfortably in a chair.

The router-table cabinet also is on wheels. The table is equipped with a router lift. The lift is offset from the center of the work surface, leaving room for drawers on one side of the cabinet to hold router bits, collet wrenches, and a laminate trimmer. Two more drawers below the router are large enough to hold another router, associated tools, and auxiliary baseplates.

Following the same design, I built rolling cabinets to hold my planer, miter saw, and tablesaw. Rather than getting stored out of sight, these cabinets fit along the walls of my shop and can be moved easily. The cabinets for these tools also have plenty of storage for any accessories.

Dust collection is easy to incorporate

The only tool in the shop that doesn't have dust collection built into its cabinet is the miter saw. Try as I might, I haven't come up with a good dust-collection system that allows me to store the cabinet against the wall. When using this tool, I usually set it up by the garage door so that the dust generated is thrown outside the shop.

To keep the shop clean, I settled on a 1-hp mobile dust collector that can be attached to one tool at a time, and it has been adequate so far.

Wheels roll in any direction and lock

securely I used four 3-in. locking swivel casters (available at hardware stores) on each rolling cabinet, which enables them to move in any direction.

When all four wheels are locked, the cabinet becomes a stable platform. Unfortunately, due primarily to its weight, moving and locking my tablesaw into place on its low cabinet was a struggle. It always seemed to go in the opposite direction I

wanted it to go. On a whim, I decided to try higher-quality, heavy-duty casters from Woodcraft Supply Corp. (www.woodcraft.com). What a difference quality makes! Not only can I move my saw with little effort, but the locking mechanism is much easier to operate.

Wall Cabinets Reduce Clutter

After taking up as much space as I could afford on the ground, I looked to the walls for more storage. I designed the wall cabinets to accommodate my work habits. I did not want deep cabinets, as things tend to get shoved to the back and become lost. I wanted my cabinets just deep enough to hold racks of storage bins. I also did not want them so high that a ladder would be necessary to access the top shelves. This led to a final dimension of 8 in. by 30 in. by 30 in. for a double-wide cabinet, and 8 in. by 15 in. by 30 in. for a single-wide cabinet.

Cars and Projects Live in Harmony

When I first came up with the idea of a small garage shop based on a mobile storage concept, I wondered how it would work out. After using the shop for more than a year, I continue to be amazed at how easy and how much fun it is to work here. All of my requirements were met, including the ability to park two vehicles in the garage when the shop is not in use.

As with any shop, there are lessons learned for building the next one. In hindsight, it would have been a good idea to plumb the workbench for dust collection and compressed air. But overall I am quite pleased with the current mix of rolling cabinets. If I do add new tools to my shop, I'll build rolling cabinets designed specifically for them.

BILL ENDRESS is an aerospace engineer in Tucson, Arizona. In his spare time, he works wood in his two-car garage.

Mobile Tools and Cabinets Improve Workflow

With the cabinets and tool stands built to corresponding heights, they can be arranged for use in a variety of combinations. The four-station arrangement shown here will accommodate a workflow that includes benchtop planing (1), ripping on the tablesaw (2), crosscutting on the miter saw (3), and routing at the router table (4). After an operation has been completed at one station, the outfeed table is rolled to the next station, where it becomes the infeed table.

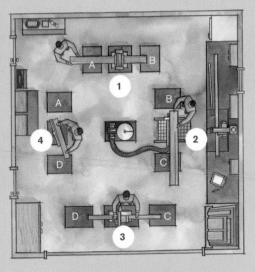

1. ROOM FOR ROUGH CUTTING. Endress starts his workflow by milling boards at the thickness planer. Rolling cabinets support the stock on its way in and out of the planer and can be moved to support boards of various lengths.

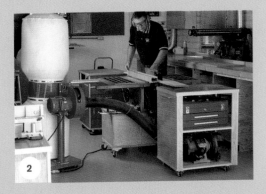

2. SUPPORT FOR LONG OR WIDE STOCK. The planer outfeed table becomes the infeed support at the tablesaw. A second cabinet catches the board on its way out.

3. INSTANT MITER-SAW STATION. Like the other power tools in this shop, the miter saw is built on a rolling cabinet designed so that the saw-cutting work surface is level with the tops of the other cabinets.

4. COMFORTABLE ROUTING STATION. After transporting a stack of freshly crosscut material from the miter saw, Endress goes to work at the router table.

Four Ways to Get Organized

BY DAVE PADGET

Woodworkers who are passionate about their craft spend a lot of time in their shops, perhaps more than in any other room of their homes. It's no surprise, then, that many woodworkers go out of their way to set up a comfortable, organized, even elegant workspace. You can tell from the way these craftsmen have set up their shops that they take great pride in their work. Following are snapshots from four shops scattered coast to coast that show the creativity of their owners. We hope they inspire you to make your shop a better place to work.

Elegant Cabinets
BY DAVE PADGET

ool storage chests and cabinets are an ancient and respected art form worthy of our best efforts. Besides their obvious usefulness, well-designed toolboxes allow craftsmen to test and demonstrate their skills. I can't help but think that these works also provide their makers with great satisfaction and enjoyment.

I know that shops are usually works in progress, constantly evolving to meet new requirements. Therefore, when designing my present shop, I tried to make things adjustable, convertible, or adaptable to mitigate the scarring of the shop that inevitably results from perpetual changes. However, I still wanted the workbench and tool cabinets to be permanent fixtures and placed them along a wall, freeing up the center of the shop for my tablesaw.

The 10-in.-deep by 144-in.-wide by 45-in.-high tool cabinet over the workbench is, without a doubt, the focal point of the shop. It features six maple raised frame-and-panel doors with walnut splined corners. The case is topped with a high crown cornice with two maple crown moldings accented with black walnut trim. The fluted pilasters separating the three sections of the cabinet have corbels at the top supporting the cornice. A small pullout shelf at the bottom of each pilaster keeps my coffee cup off the workbench. One of

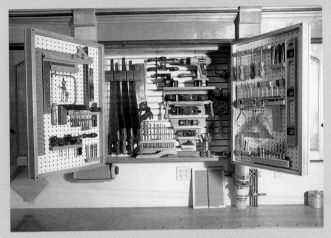

T-SLOTTED PANELS, COMMON IN RETAIL DISPLAYS, ARE USED INSIDE THE CABINETS. Custom-made tool holders fit into the slots. The backs of the doors are fitted with pegboard.

the pilasters houses a 4-in. dust-collection duct.

Inside the cabinet my tools are hung on T-slotted panels (commonly seen in retail displays). These panels are for mounting fixtures and require a metal bracket that slips into the slot. They are durable, stable, and easily adapted to a variety of needs. The panels and the metal brackets can be ordered from commercial retail merchandising distributors.

A workbench often is called upon to handle tasks other than woodworking. Tools such as lawnmowers and chainsaws aren't kind to a maple benchtop. That's why I covered 5 ft. of my 12-ft.-long bench with a stainless-steel cap.

SOLID-WOOD CABINETS DRESS UP THE SHOP. Padget loves spending time in his shop, and he's made it as elegant as the rest of his home.

Elegant Cabinets (cont.)

The woodworking section of my bench is laminated maple with a maple face and end vises with walnut handles and walnut benchdogs. There is also a bench slave on the right leg to support long material while in the face vise. The bench features raised frame-and-panel ends and fluted pilaster legs. A maple storage cabinet under the work surface houses drawers with black walnut sides dovetailed to maple faces and sliding maple tills with walnut splined corners. The bench also is equipped with 110-volt and 220-volt power, high-pressure air, and a vacuum.

Elsewhere in the shop I have two rolling storage units (one vertical, one horizontal) for sheet goods. These units have heavy-duty hinges on one side attached to the wall or adjoining cabinet. Two 3-in. heavy-duty casters on the other end support the outward end off the floor and allow the unit to be swung or rolled out from the wall for easy access to the contents. It can be pushed back against the wall and out of the way. One of the rolling units can be made from a 12-ft. 2x10 and one 4x8 sheet of plywood. I mounted the vertical unit on the side of the clamp-storage closet. The horizontal unit is mounted to a wall

SWIVELING VERTICAL STORAGE UNIT. One edge is fastened to the wall with heavy hinges, and casters underneath allow the unit to pivot for easy access.

shelf support. All of the shelving in my shop is attached to the walls rather than standing on the floor (saving precious floor space) and is totally adjustable.

The pursuit of shop storage perfection will go on and on because it is as individualized as each woodworker. The important thing is to engage in and enjoy the creative process.

DAVE PADGET works wood in Olympia, Washington.

Movable Tool Racks
BY CARL SWENSSON

I work in a cinder-block basement shop and, needless to say, the walls are not pretty. I've partly solved this problem and answered the question of how to store most of my hand tools by building simple tool racks out of clear pine. The racks lend a warm touch to an otherwise visually cold working environment.

The racks are hung on French cleats, which allow me to move a whole set of tools to where I'm working in the shop. I went a little overboard by gluing up blocking to the front of the cleats (and to the front of the lower spacer blocks as well) to create breadboard ends. The blocking extends a hair beyond the face of the rack and produces a shadow line, which lends a finished look.

This simple tool-rack design is practical for many reasons. First, I know where every tool is at a glance. Because the most-used tools are so easily and conveniently stored, I'm less apt to let them pile up and clutter my bench when working.

To add or subtract tools from the racks, all I need is a claw hammer and a fistful of nails. Although you can hang a lot of tools just by a nail alone, I did make a number of wooden holders for things like chisels and hammers. Most of these holders are simple blocks of wood with notched holes that allow a tool to be slipped into the holder without having to raise it very far and bump into other tools placed above. If you design your holders so that tools must be lifted up and out, you have to leave room above, which wastes space.

Last, I've noticed that when my customers visit my shop, they enjoy seeing this orderly display of tools. It gives them a sense of what is needed to create a piece of furniture.

CARL SWENSSON designs furniture and teaches woodworking.

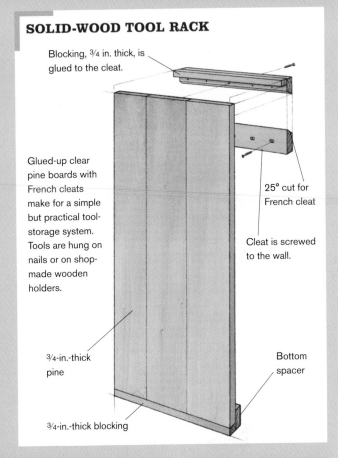

SOLID-WOOD TOOL RACK

Blocking, ¾ in. thick, is glued to the cleat.

Glued-up clear pine boards with French cleats make for a simple but practical tool-storage system. Tools are hung on nails or on shop-made wooden holders.

25° cut for French cleat

Cleat is screwed to the wall.

¾-in.-thick pine

¾-in.-thick blocking

Bottom spacer

SWENSSON USES CLEAR PINE BOARDS FOR TOOL RACKS. **The pine is a warm, pleasant alternative to the drab, cinder-block walls of his shop.**

IT'S EASY TO RECONFIGURE A TOOL RACK. **Just pull out the nails and start over.**

Using Wasted Space

BY FRED SOTCHER

A well-designed storage system makes it easy to find tools and hardware, allows for flexibility as needs change, and makes the best use of limited space. It also should be low in cost, look good, and show off the more attractive tools. I have a variety of storage systems in my basement shop that meet these requirements.

I've never seen storage cabinets that hang out over part of the tablesaw. But that's exactly what I built. My cabinets fill the wasted space to the right and rear of the blade and store jigs for the saw. Doors on both ends let in enough light for me to find things easily. The cabinets are set far enough out of the way that I never run into a problem when cutting tenons or other tall parts.

You hardly ever see glass-faced cabinets in workshops, but I built some anyway. In the 10 years since, I have yet to break one pane of glass. I did mount them rather high, at about the same level you would install kitchen cabinets. I can spot what I need from halfway across the room.

If you have a set of stairs leading into your shop, build shelves or pullout drawers to fit under the treads. You'd be surprised at how much stuff can be put away in this awkward space.

There are a lot of small items that need to be stored in the average workshop, including screws, hinges, template rings for routers, and replacement parts. Instead of tossing them in drawers or on shelves where they will get mixed up, I use jars, plastic storage bins, and what are known as stock boxes, cardboard storage bins that you can buy from industrial suppliers such as Grainger (888-361-8649) and MSC (800-645-7270).

I like to have my hand and power tools within easy reach. For them, I built angled (set at 15 degrees) display racks. I screwed French cleats to the faces of the racks to hang specially designed tool holders. Heavy tools have dedicated holders. This system allows me to reconfigure the racks as needed.

FRED SOTCHER is a retired electrical engineer who works wood in San Jose, California.

OVERHEAD CABINETS RESIDE ABOVE THE TABLESAW. Sotcher likes glass-door panels (at left in photo) because they make it a lot easier to locate tools. And he says he has not broken one pane in 10 years.

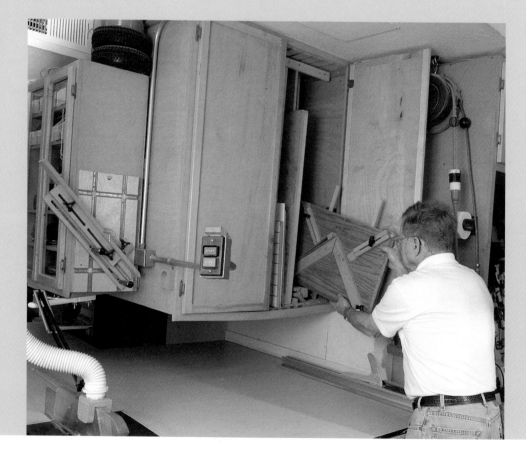

ADJUSTABLE WOOD STORAGE RACK. The rack is converted from horizontal storage to vertical storage by simply removing the cross pieces.

ANGLED TOOL RACKS ARE PLACED ABOVE THE BENCH. Individual tool holders are attached to the rack with French cleats.

Revolving Tool Rack
BY JOE JOHNS

Whether your shop is large or small, and your tool collection miserly or princely, it is satisfying to figure out storage solutions that are efficient, adaptable, and inexpensive. Now, I don't have anything against pegboard, but frankly, pegboard is boring. I like to show off my creativity in the shop as well as in my woodworking. That's why I designed a swiveling tool rack.

My tool rack makes highly efficient use of wall space. It takes up only about 15 sq. ft. but returns 40 sq. ft. of storage (both sides of the panels are usable). The panels don't bump into each other because they're all linked via sprockets by a length of chain.

The construction of the panels couldn't be simpler. They consist of ½-in.-thick medium-density overlay (which is fir plywood covered with paper), surrounded by a 2-in.-thick frame of medium-density fiberboard. Each panel is centered on a metal pin attached to a sprocket connected to a length of chain. A second pin is attached to the top of each panel frame. I fitted my panels between upper and lower cabinets (the pins on the frames fit into matching holes in the cabinets). But to simplify things, you could fit the panels between a pair of L-shaped plywood support brackets bolted to the wall. Be sure to use lag bolts and tap into the studs. For tool holders, I drilled holes in the panels to accept lengths of wooden dowels and steel rods. It's easiest to do this with the tools arranged on a panel laid flat.

JOE JOHNS lives in Ronan, Montana, where he specializes in furniture design, antique repair and refinishing, and custom cabinetry.

BIRD'S-EYE VIEW OF THE TOOL RACK

With a revolving tool rack, both sides of each panel can be put to use. And with so many tools out in the open, it's a lot easier and faster to find what you are looking for.

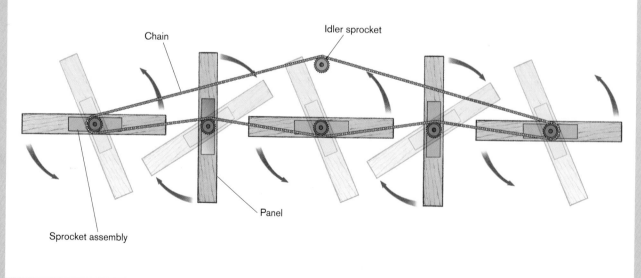

Chain

Idler sprocket

Panel

Sprocket assembly

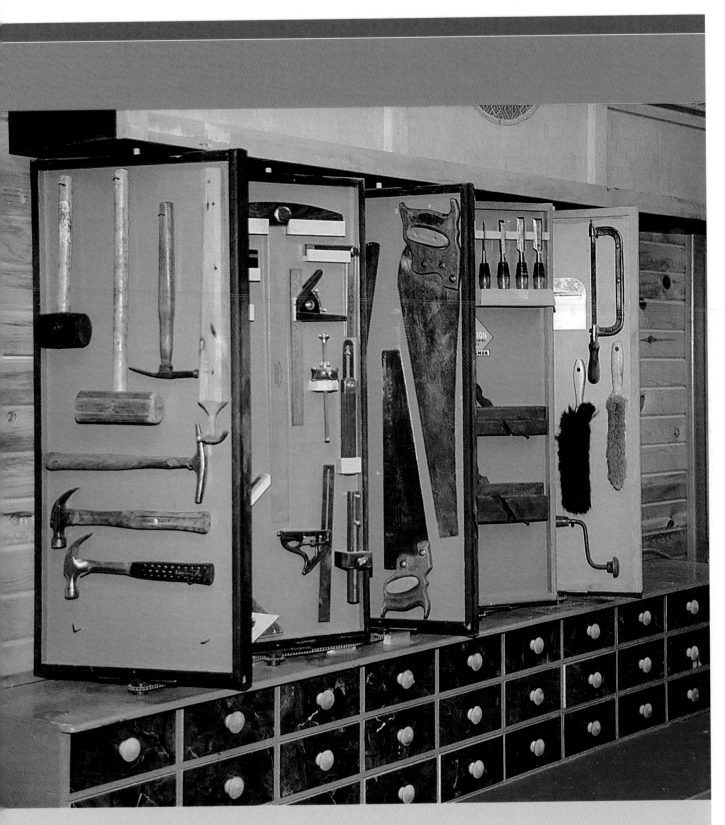

FIVE-PANEL TOOL RACK REVOLVES. Johns's tool rack provides about 40 sq. ft. of storage while taking up only 15 sq. ft. of wall space.

Clamp Storage Solutions

BY JOHN WEST

Clamps are to woodshops what closets are to houses: You can't have too many of them. Band clamps, bar clamps, C-clamps, corner clamps, edge clamps, hand clamps, miter clamps, pipe clamps, quick clamps, spring clamps—you can pile them all in a corner or throw them into a drawer. Or you can organize them on a wall or a movable cart that will make them easy to get at when you need them and will keep them out of the way when you don't. What follows are examples of how some of our readers solved their clamp-storage problems.

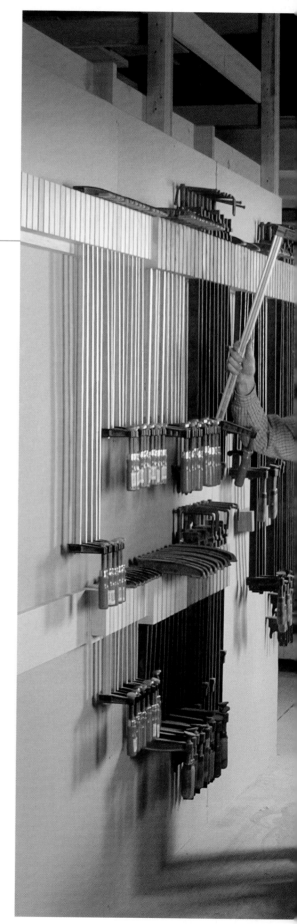

Wall Rack

BY JOHN WEST

Having recently moved to a smaller shop, I had to find somewhere to store my fairly large collection of bar clamps and hand clamps. When considering where to put them, I decided against a fancy rack that rolls around the shop on casters because the floor space it would require is too dear. I wanted my clamps near the area where large glue-up projects will be done, but I also wanted to keep them out of the way when they're not needed. The solution was to hang the clamps on the outside wall of a lumber-storage rack. (In the business world, they call this "multitasking.")

The racks I designed are quite simple, and they can be used to store a variety of different-size clamps. First, securely fasten a ¾-in.-thick hanger strip (plywood or medium-density fiberboard) to the wall, using two screws at every stud location. This hanger strip serves two purposes: It's a sturdy anchor, and it adds depth for building out the rack enough to make a good ledge on which to hang the bar clamps. Along the bottom of the hanger strip goes another ¾-in. plywood cleat (what some people call a French cleat) with a 45-degree cut along the top edge. That bottom cleat gets screwed to the hanger cleat. Another matching plywood cleat with a 45-degree cut along the bottom edge has blocks of lumber screwed into the front face from behind; these blocks are spaced apart so there's room to hang the clamps on them. Nothing fancy—most of the racks I used were salvaged from my previous shop, where they've given 20 years of faithful service so far. Depending on the type of clamps, they will hang better facing in or out, because of how the weight is balanced. On the 12-ft. wall shown on the facing page, I currently store 108 clamps, and there's room for more.

JOHN WEST owns and operates Cope and Mould Millwork in Ridgefield, Connecticut.

BAR-CLAMP RACK

By hanging all of his clamps on one wall, West can space the hanging racks apart as necessary to fit different sizes of clamps. The deep-throat bar clamps face outward; the more traditional, older-style bar clamps face the wall. This rack was made longer to allow room for a growing collection of clamps.

Mounting detail

Top cleat, ¾-in.-thick plywood

Blocks, 1½ in. thick by 2 in. wide by 6 in. long, are screwed into the top cleat.

Hanger strip, ¾-in.-thick plywood or MDF, is screwed through the wall and into studs.

⅜ in. between blocks

After hanging the top cleat, drive additional screws into the hanger strip.

Bottom cleat with 45° edge is screwed to the hanger strip.

Insulation, Vapor Barrier, Then Plywood

INSULATION TO KEEP YOUR TOES WARM. In colder climates, place rigid insulation between the rows of sleepers.

SHEETING PROVIDES A VAPOR BARRIER. Spread 6-mil. polyethylene sheeting across the top of the sleepers and insulation. Cover the whole space, and if you need more than one sheet, overlap seams by 6 in.

GET THE FIRST PIECE RIGHT. Take your time placing the first plywood sheet because all of the other pieces will follow its course. Be sure to leave a ½-in. gap at the walls around the perimeter to give the plywood some room to expand.

to the wall. Leave a gap of ½ in. all the way around to give the plywood a little breathing room. You can cover the gap with a piece of baseboard or shoe molding.

Finishing the floor is a matter of personal preference. A coat or two of paint or clear finish will help protect the plywood from the inevitable coffee or paint spill. But for a shop, that may be more trouble than it's worth. Your feet, knees, ankles, and back—as well as your edge tools—will be just as happy with an unfinished floor.

SCOTT GIBSON, a contributing editor to *Fine Homebuilding*, lives in Maine.

Shop Flooring Solutions

BY ANATOLE BURKIN

Concrete is a perfect shop floor for machines. But it's not so kind to the body or to the occasional dropped hand tool. Concrete is especially nasty in the winter if your shop is in a detached building. And no matter how high the indoor-air temperature gets, the floor is always cold, even in warmer months.

Determined to get off the slab and to do it with a minimum of fuss, I surveyed what floor coverings were available. My primary goal was to find products that would be easy to install and would keep my feet from freezing in winter. Of secondary importance was to find products that acted as a moisture barrier, could protect a dropped tool, and were easy to keep moderately clean.

I found five types of flooring products that seemed to meet all of those criteria. One is a wood composite; the others are PVC based.

Wood Composite vs. PVC

The wood-composite product, called DRI-core®, is a subflooring material made of random waferboard bonded to a high-density polyethylene base. This tongue-and-groove product was created as a base for carpet, vinyl tile, or engineered hardwood flooring, but it may be used as is. The color

PVC Tiles

Available in a variety of colors and sizes, PVC tiles have interlocking tabs, some of which create almost invisible seams. Quick to install and ready for immediate use, these tiles lend a bright and modern look to a concrete floor.

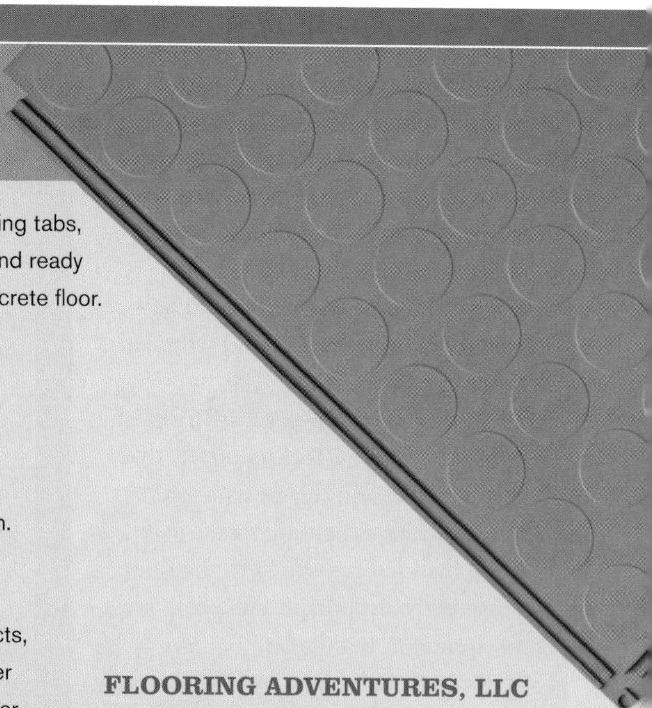

LOCK-TILE®

Evertile Flooring Co.
888-562-5845
www.locktile-usa.com
Lock-tile pieces are ¼ in. thick and 19⅝ in. square. They come in nine colors (custom colors may be ordered but only in large quantities). Like other PVC-tile products, these can be installed with a rubber mallet and a utility knife. The interlocking tabs create a snug but exposed joint.
Approximate cost: $3.20 per sq. ft.

FLOORING ADVENTURES, LLC

877-779-2454
www.flooringadventures.com
Tuff-Seal Advanced interlocking floor tiles are ¼ in. thick and 18 in. square and come in seven colors. The hidden interlocking dovetail-shaped tabs seemed to be the best-designed joint of all the samples; the connection is secure and nearly invisible, leaving only a hairline gap between adjoining tiles.
Approximate cost: $4.39 per sq. ft.

BOTTOM

BOTTOM

LOCKING TABS VARY IN STYLE. Lock-tile tabs leave a visible seam (above), whereas Century tiles have tabs that join in a tight, clean, and hidden seam (right).

BOTTOM

RESILIA

FloorSurfaces Inc.

www.floorsurfaces.com

Resilia interlocking tiles come in a choice of 20 colors, and for a surcharge, custom colors may be ordered. These ¼-in.-thick tiles are 12 in. square and have a hidden interlocking joint, which leaves only a hairline seam between tiles. Approximate cost: $3.45 per sq. ft.

A CLEAN LOOK. When locked together, the Resillia tiles have a tight seam.

LAYING PVC FLOORING

THE TIGHT INTERLOCKING TABS ARE JOINED EASILY WITH A MALLET. Knock the interlocking edges into place with a rubber mallet for a snug, flush seam.

TRIM THE TILES WITH A UTILITY KNIFE AND A STRAIGHTEDGE. **PVC tiles are thin enough to be cut to size with a standard utility knife.**

A CLEAN FINISH. Some manufacturers offer edge strips, which are snapped on or glued into place.

minor damage, except for the Better Life Technology PVC sheet, which was partially punctured. Such a fine slit, however, is unlikely to degrade the product.

I dabbed each type of flooring product with typical shop chemicals such as naphtha, alcohol, and oil stain, and did not see any damage (the PVC products are rated against damage from a host of chemicals). Except for the DRIcore tiles, which absorbed some stain, all of the flooring samples cleaned up easily.

What to Choose for Your Shop

It seems you couldn't go wrong with any of these flooring products, based on the ease of installation and the insulation improvement. Budget, however, may be a factor in your decision (prices are noted in the comments about the individual products), as may be aesthetic considerations. For instance, the PVC flooring comes in numerous colors. You could even make a checkerboard pattern if you go with the PVC tiles. PVC also is a durable substance, and it might wear better than wood composite.

There's another point worth mentioning: During the course of my review, a number of people asked me which of the flooring products was more comfortable to stand on. I can't say any of them is a substitute for antifatigue mats, which have a lot more give. But I did appreciate the insulating qualities that the DRIcore tiles provided during cold weather.

ANATOLE BURKIN is the publisher of *Fine Woodworking* and an avid woodworker.

PVC Rolls

This material covers a concrete floor in no time, lending a clean and uniform covering. Although durable, it is thinner and more flexible than the PVC tiles.

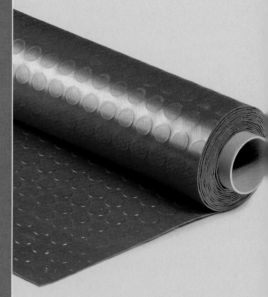

BLT (BETTER LIFE TECHNOLOGY)

877-810-6444

www.bltllc.com

BLT's PVC floor covering comes in a roll. The material is about 1/8 in. thick and is available in various widths and lengths and in six colors. BLT's covering is the easiest product to install: Simply unroll it. Adjoining sheets can be butted together, but for a better joint, tape mating edges to the concrete with indoor/outdoor double-faced tape.

Approximate cost: $1.10 per sq. ft.

Rolling Out PVC Flooring

COVER A LARGE SURFACE AREA IN NO TIME. The large, heavy rolls are easy to install once in position. Wait for warm weather, as the PVC material is more pliable and easier to unroll above 60°F.

TRIM WITH A UTILITY KNIFE. Before trimming the excess material, allow it to relax at the base of the wall.

HOLD DOWN EDGES WITH TAPE. When taping the edges, use indoor/outdoor double-faced tape.

Heating Your Shop

BY ANDY ENGEL

My first woodworking shop was in a garage in northern New Jersey. I cobbled together some insulation, weatherstripping, and an old woodstove to make the shop mostly habitable—for me. For my tools and projects, though, I suspect it was a hostile environment. Morning often found the shop below freezing, which precluded storing glue or waterborne finishes there. Stoking the stove quickly launched the mercury into the 80s, a fluctuation in temperature and humidity that did my lumber no good. And, if the shop remained unused for any length of time during the winter, rust bloomed on my tools.

Better insulation and a heater I was comfortable burning in my absence would have fixed the problems. I think 50°F is good for an empty shop, and with decent insulation and air sealing, it's a temperature that shouldn't cost an arm and a leg to maintain in most climates.

Dust and Fumes Can Be a Hazard

Wood dust will burn at 500°F or less, and clouds of dust can ignite if they're exposed to hot surfaces or an open flame. Aside from the fire risk, even relatively minor

Locating Your Heat Source

A heater must be safe, unobtrusive, close enough to warm you, but not so close as to roast you. Locating it between you and a door or window often works, because the heater can warm the cold air these openings admit.

Wall mount
Often an easy option, the electric heaters require no venting, and the fuel-fired models vent through a small hole in the wall. One downside is that they occupy often scarce wall space.

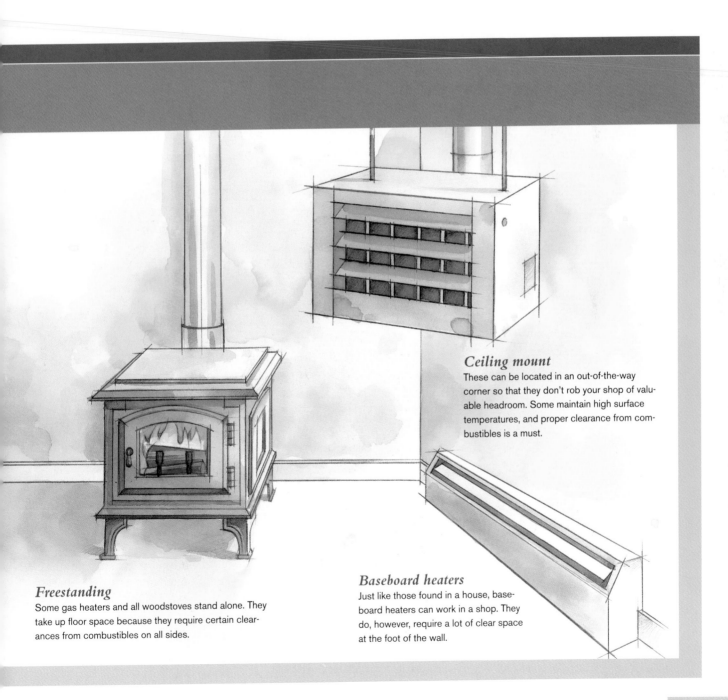

Ceiling mount

These can be located in an out-of-the-way corner so that they don't rob your shop of valuable headroom. Some maintain high surface temperatures, and proper clearance from combustibles is a must.

Freestanding

Some gas heaters and all woodstoves stand alone. They take up floor space because they require certain clearances from combustibles on all sides.

Baseboard heaters

Just like those found in a house, baseboard heaters can work in a shop. They do, however, require a lot of clear space at the foot of the wall.

Fuel for Thought

The type of fuel that's most convenient is a big factor in choosing a heater. Fuel prices are volatile, so the discussion of price here, although based on history, is quite general.

NATURAL GAS

Natural gas, piped under city streets, is a good choice, particularly if your house is hooked up already. Gas is usually moderately priced, although it's a commodity, so the price fluctuates with demand. You buy it as you use it, so you can't stockpile fuel in the summer, when prices tend to drop. Because gas burns very cleanly, heater maintenance is minimal. And because it's supplied from a pipeline, you never run out.

PROPANE

Propane burns in the same appliances as natural gas. However, because propane contains more Btu per given volume, it's critical that your heater is set up to burn it. With most heaters, that's a simple matter. Propane is delivered to a tank outside that you either buy or rent from the supplier. It's generally more expensive per Btu than natural gas, and rarely is used where natural gas is available. Filling up at cheaper summer prices can save money. Propane heaters are also low maintenance.

KEROSENE AND FUEL OIL

Kerosene and #1 and #2 fuel oil are readily available in the Northeast and Northwest, less so in other parts of the country. Their cost per Btu generally ends up the cheapest. Like propane, they're stored on site in a tank that you own. Prices are often lower in the summer. Unlike gas, kerosene- and oil-burning heaters need a cleaning and a tune-up every year or so, a cost that should be factored in. In a cold climate, oil may still be cheapest. In more moderate climates, this cost might give gas the edge.

ELECTRICITY

Electricity is simple: Pay the bill every month and it keeps on coming. With no flue or piping to run, electric heaters are cheap to install and don't require regular maintenance. Depending on your electricity rates, however, they can be the most expensive to run.

WOOD

Wood is tempting. After all, most of us have scrap that sure looks like free heat. The amount of wood it takes to get through a winter can be surprising, though. If you spend any serious time in the shop, you likely will need to lay in some cordwood. And if you are not in the shop every day to fire it up, keeping minimal heat going with a woodstove is dicey.

shop dust encrusting any type of heater will make it less efficient.

There are two types of fuel-burning appliances. Open-combustion appliances, such as woodstoves or gas heaters with pilot lights, feed the flame with air from inside the room and are potential ignition sources in dusty environments. Sealed-combustion appliances, such as most direct-vent kerosene heaters and many gas heaters, have no connection between the combustion chamber and the inside air. Rather, a supply duct brings air from outside into the chamber to support the flame. These are safer.

As a practical matter, a woodworker who installs a decent dust-collection system probably will never create enough airborne dust to make the atmosphere truly risky. Most types of heaters should be safe to use in a shop as long as you collect the dust, don't allow flammable fumes to build up, and clean off the heater on a regular basis. To limit the risk, ask the manufacturer if the surface temperature of the heater will

Closed Combustion Is Safe and Efficient

In a closed-combustion heater, air for combustion is drawn in from the outside, rather than from the heated space. This offers several advantages, the first of which is safety. Because there is no flame exposed to the shop air, the chance of flammable vapors, say from a lacquer-thinner spill, encountering an ignition source is greatly reduced.

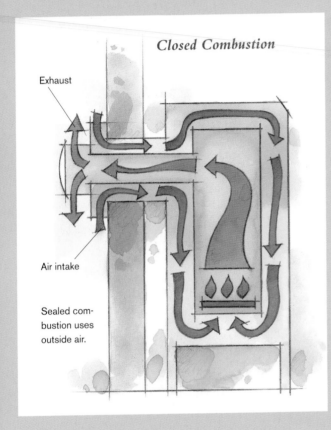

Closed Combustion

Exhaust

Air intake

Sealed combustion uses outside air.

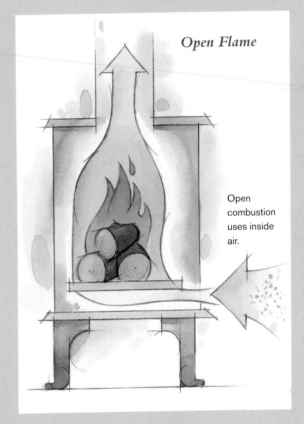

Open Flame

Open combustion uses inside air.

exceed 500°F or if there's an open flame. It's a good idea to check with your building inspector and your property-insurance agent before you install heat in a shop.

Although their simplicity may be tempting, avoid any unvented fuel-burning appliance in the shop. Unvented kerosene heaters in particular don't work well when their wicks become contaminated with wood dust. And when they aren't burning efficiently, kerosene heaters produce carbon monoxide, which can cause health problems even at low concentrations. Lacking a wick, gas burners aren't as sensitive to dust as kerosene heaters. Both types produce water as a by-product, which means an unvented fuel-burning heater will increase the moisture in your shop. If the heater stays off in your absence, this moisture is likely to condense, and no doubt will rust the costliest tool in your arsenal.

How Heat Moves

Heat warms a building by radiation and convection. Neither is inherently better, and neither works alone. Convection heaters radiate some heat, and radiant heaters create convective loops.

RADIANT HEAT

Radiation is the transfer of heat via electromagnetic waves, such as the infrared waves radiated by a woodstove. Radiation travels through the air, but doesn't warm it much. Rather, it transfers its heat to solid bodies, such as you or your tablesaw. As these solid bodies warm, they will heat the surrounding air, creating some convection. However, most of the warmth you feel from a radiant source is infrared, and has nothing to do with air temperature.

CONVECTION

Convection is the transfer of heat by a moving fluid, which in this case means air. Forced-air heaters are convective heaters that work by surrounding you with warm air.

CONVECTIVE LOOP

As air warmed by a heat source rises, it sucks in cool air from below to replace it, forming a loop of gently moving air. To heat a large area, the heater needs a big surface area, such as a baseboard. Where space is tight, passive radiant heaters may not be the best choice.

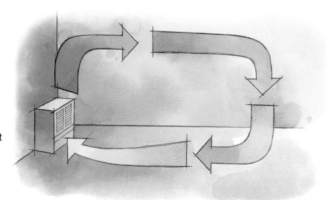

Buy Insulation Once, Save Fuel Forever

The first step to heating a shop is matching the insulation level to the climate. Remember, you buy insulation once, but fuel costs go on forever. Do it right. That said, the details of shop insulation are beyond the scope of this chapter. Your local building code will specify the minimum insulation values for residential construction, and these are a good place to start. You can always add more insulation than code requires; doing so will increase your comfort and decrease your energy usage. However, it will probably take a long time to recoup the cost of extra insulation if you go far beyond the code requirements.

Air sealing is at least as important as the R-value (resistance to heat flow) of your insulation. In a drafty cavity, most insulation has an R-value of close to zero. Any breach in the building envelope—be it a door without weatherstripping, a leaky attic hatch, or a hole in a wall—will cost you heat and money all out of proportion to the hole size. Pay particular attention to the ceiling and the tops of the wall framing. Because warm air rises, you can almost watch the dollar bills floating out of the smallest holes in these areas. Garage doors need close attention as well.

After insulating your shop, figure out just how much heat you need. Here's where a knowledgeable supplier can be a great help. Heater size depends on the climate, the size and insulation level of the shop, and how warm you want to be. For example, a two-car garage shop insulated to residential standards in southern Connecticut would require about 30,000 Btu of heat per hour on an average winter day.

The downside of an undersize heating system is obvious—you'll be cold. Oversize systems aren't good, either, because they don't deliver consistent heat. They kick on at the right temperature, but quickly make it hotter than the thermostat setting, causing big swings in temperature. This is called short cycling, and it's not only uncomfortable, but the constant starts and stops are bad for the equipment's longevity and efficiency. And bigger equipment costs more. Forced to choose between undersizing and oversizing, I'd undersize, and get through the coldest days with a portable electric heater.

Two Ways to Feel Warm: Convection vs. Radiant Heat

Heat reaches the occupants of a building in one of two main ways: convection, which for this purpose is the movement of warm air; or radiation, the kind of heat you feel when standing next to a campfire. Forced-air heaters work by convection. Most other heaters work mainly by radiation or a combination of the two mechanisms.

Forced-air heat warms a space quickly, but because it warms the entire space, it might cost more to run. Radiant heaters can be set up to warm specific areas, such as your workbench, leaving the rest of your shop cooler. That said, as the radiant heat warms solid objects such as your bench and tablesaw, they in turn warm the air. The effectiveness of radiant heat varies with the surface area of the radiant source, the temperature of the source, and the distance from the source.

ANDY ENGEL splits his time between writing and working as a home energy consultant, remodeling contractor, and architectural woodworker.

The heater you choose will be determined by some combination of where you can put it, the fuel, and how the heat moves. Shown here are some common types with their pros, cons, and costs. When considering cost, don't forget installation. An extreme do-it-yourselfer could install any of these heaters, but most of us would hire a pro for at least part of the job.

GAS-FIRED HEATERS
LOCATION: wall, floor
FUEL: natural gas, propane
COMBUSTION: sealed
HEAT TYPE: convection

Most wall heaters are surface mounted, and vent outside through the wall via a horizontal flue. Gravity furnaces are one type: Tall and thin, they suck in cold air from the floor level and vent it out the top. An optional blower can improve airflow. These heaters come in sizes from 10,000 Btu to 50,000 Btu, and cost in the range of $400 to $800.

Counterflow furnaces are similar, except that an internal fan reverses the natural upward flow of heated air within the furnace, blowing warm air out of a louvre near the floor. Priced between $800 and $1,200, these are available up to 65,000 Btu.

Console-type heaters are lower and wider, similar in size to a woodstove, with an output of 20,000 Btu to 70,000 Btu. Their price range is $500 to $900.

Manufacturers include Louisville Tin and Stove Co. (www.cozyheaters.com), Empire Comfort Systems (www.empirecomfort.com), and Rinnai (www.rinnai.us). Major furnace manufacturers such as Trane® and York® also make counterflow furnaces.

ELECTRIC HEATERS
LOCATION: wall
FUEL: electricity
COMBUSTION: none
HEAT TYPE: radiant, convection

Probably the simplest heater to install and the least expensive to buy is the wall-mount electric heater. There are two types: those that use a fan to force air over electric resistance coils and into the shop, and those that heat by radiation or by creating a natural convective current. They're available in small sizes (500 watts), or in larger units (8,000 watts). The small ones run on 120v, the larger on 240v. Expect to pay from $100–$800 depending on size. Installation is relatively simple, requiring mainly a dedicated electrical circuit. The downside is that even the larger models produce only the equivalent of about 24,000 Btu, suitable for a one-car garage in a cold climate. Manufacturers include TPI Corp. (www.tpicorp.com), Marley Engineered Products (www.marleymeh.com), Cadet (www.cadetco.com), and Empire Comfort (www.empirecomfort.com).

OIL-FIRED HEATERS
LOCATION: wall, floor
FUEL: kerosene, heating oil
COMBUSTION: sealed
HEAT TYPE: convection

Another through-the-wall option is a unit that burns kerosene or stove oil (#1 low-sulphur heating oil). Units that burn #2 home heating oil are available, but need more regular maintenance. Oil-fired heaters claim high efficiencies and the lowest cost per Btu, but require an outside fuel tank. Outside tanks can be problematic in really cold weather, because cold fuel oil can gel. Additives are available to prevent this problem, but you have to remember to add them. The only wall penetrations are a small hole for the flue and the outside combustion-air intake, and an even smaller hole for the fuel line. Sizes range from 15,000 Btu to 43,000 Btu, prices from $750 to $1,600.

Manufacturers include Monitor Products (www.monitorproducts.com) and Toyotomi (www.toyostove.com).

FAN-FORCED HEATERS

LOCATION: ceiling
FUEL: multi
COMBUSTION: varies
HEAT TYPE: convection

Several manufacturers make fan-forced, gas-fired units that hang from above. The cost hovers around $500, and the Btu range is from 30,000 to 75,000. Add the cost for the flue and the electric and gas hookup.

Fan-forced hot-water (hydronic) heaters are also available. Because no part of the heater ever gets hotter than the water, there is no fire danger. The downside is the need for a hot-water source. In a shop attached to a house with hot-water heat, you might tap into the existing system. You'll have to keep the shop above freezing or run a special antifreeze through the heating system. These heaters start at around $350, but piping adds to the cost. If you have to add a boiler, the cost will run into the thousands. Sizes range from 18,000 Btu to close to a million Btu. Manufacturers include Modine (www.modine.com) and Marley Engineered Products (www.marleymeh.com).

WOOD STOVES

LOCATION: floor
FUEL: wood, pellets
COMBUSTION: open
HEAT TYPE: radiant

Wood stoves can be the ultimate in cheap heat, or a nuisance. Because there's always an open flame, the danger of fire never really goes away. Building codes require at least 3 ft. of clearance to combustibles and a noncombustible hearth that extends at least 18 in. from the stove. Stoves require an annual chimney sweeping and regular ash cleanout. A big advantage to a woodworker is that they also get rid of scrap. And woodstoves are the only option mentioned here that don't release greenhouse gases. They can emit substantial particulate matter, however. Check if your town regulates such emissions before installation. Pellet stoves are a costlier option. A thermostatically controlled hopper feeds cellulose pellets into the stove as needed. Pellets aren't free, but the convenience is a valuable consideration.

INFRARED HEATERS

LOCATION: ceiling
FUEL: gas, electric
COMBUSTION: sealed
HEAT TYPE: radiant

Often called infrared heaters, these are either gas-fired or electric. Smaller units can provide spot heating over a workbench; several can heat an entire shop.

The smallest gas-fired model is 25,000 Btu and costs about $650. Be sure you get a model certified for residential use, such as Detroit Radiant's LS or LD series (www.reverber ray.com), or Schwank's STR 45-10 (www.schwankheaters.com) if you're heating an attached garage. One downside is the high surface temperature. You need at least an 8-ft. ceiling for a gas-fired radiant heater. And you need to maintain the clearances to combustible materials specified by the manufacturer.

Electric radiant heaters don't suffer from the same clearance constraints as gas units. One manufacturer, Ennerjoy (www.sshcinc.com) targets the woodshop market by selling panels with slight cosmetic defects for $250 for a 1,000-watt unit.

HEAT PUMPS

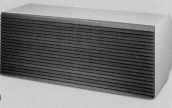

LOCATION: wall
FUEL: electric
COMBUSTION: none
HEAT TYPE: convection

A through-the-wall heat pump is another electrically powered option. Commonly used in hotel rooms, heat pumps work like refrigerators or air conditioners, extracting the heat from the air and moving it somewhere else. The chief advantage of heat pumps is that they can be set to cool the air as well. They're available in sizes from about 7,000 Btu to 15,000 Btu, and are best suited to moderate climates. For cold weather, many heat pumps have auxiliary electric coils that kick in and produce heat. Costs run from $500 to $1,000. Manufacturers include most major HVAC suppliers.

Lighting for the Workshop

BY JACK L. LINDSEY

The owner of a small shop can seldom justify the services of a lighting design professional. So the task of lighting a shop is usually accomplished by putting up a few fixtures and, if that doesn't work, adding a few more. Sometimes this works, but learning some of the basics about lighting will produce better results faster and more economically in the long run. The most common mistakes are using the wrong type of lamp or fixture, installing too few fixtures, and putting fixtures in the wrong locations.

The first step in lighting a shop is to decide what strategy to use: To light the whole shop in a reasonably uniform manner or to concentrate light at machines and work areas.

For small shops, I recommend uniform lighting because it allows you the freedom to change the location of machines and workstations within the shop. It also means you can install fluorescent fixtures in continuous rows. This reduces the cost of electrical wiring by allowing you to run wires through the fixtures instead of installing a separate feed to each fixture. If you take this approach, wires are run within 3 in. of the ballast, so you must use wire that is rated for 90°C.

Fixtures

Two basic types of fluorescent fixtures, called strips or industrials, are commonly used for shop lighting. Strip fixtures are simply metal channels fitted with lamp holders and ballasts. For really tight spaces, you can use a low-profile strip fixture with lamps mounted on the sides of the fixture instead of the bottom. Industrial fixtures are equipped with a white metal reflector mounted above the lamps.

Strips should be used when fixtures are mounted directly to a finished ceiling that has been painted flat white. Industrials work better when the ceiling is not flat or not painted white, or when fixtures must be suspended below the ceiling.

Industrial fixtures are available in two types—apertured and nonapertured. Apertured fixtures have a series of holes in the reflector that allow air to pass through, which helps keep lamp and fixture surfaces clean. Also, air circulation cools the ballast, thus extending its working lifetime. A ballast in an apertured fixture can easily last twice as long as one in a nonapertured fixture.

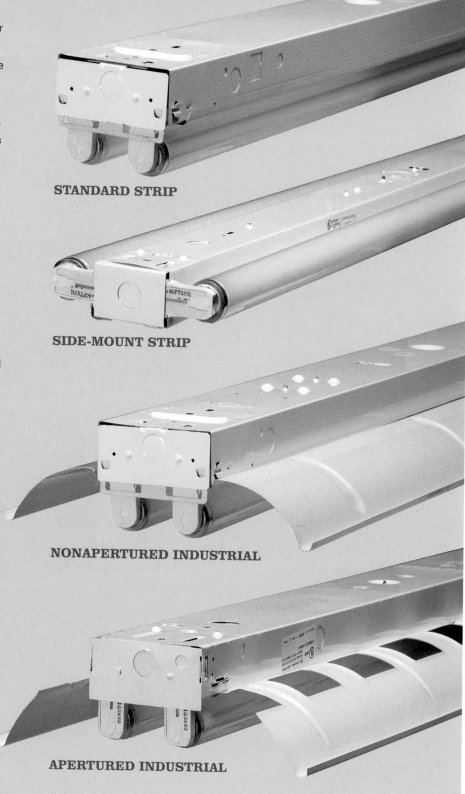

STANDARD STRIP

SIDE-MOUNT STRIP

NONAPERTURED INDUSTRIAL

APERTURED INDUSTRIAL

Placement

The older you are and the more detailed the work you do, the more light you need. Concentrated spot or task lighting works, but a uniformly lit space, like the one shown at right, will allow you more flexibility and improve your working environment.

Here are the steps for determining the placement of light fixtures:

1. Measure the distance between the light source and the horizontal work surface (X).

2. The distance between rows of fixtures (Y) should be a maximum of 1½ times the distance X.

3. The distance between a wall and a row of fixtures (Z) should be approximately a third to half the distance Y.

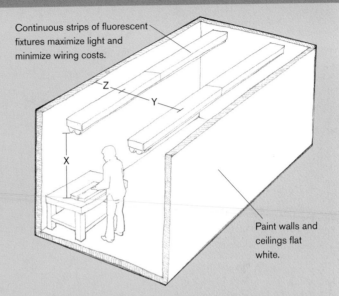

Continuous strips of fluorescent fixtures maximize light and minimize wiring costs.

Paint walls and ceilings flat white.

Here is a breakdown of how many two-lamp, 8-ft. fluorescent fixtures you will need to light a workshop uniformly to 100 fc of light. For 4-ft. fixtures, just double the numbers in the chart. Consult a qualified electrician to determine the size and number of circuits required to power your lighting needs.

CALCULATING HOW MANY YOU NEED

Room size	Energy saving 60 watt	Full wattage 75 watt	High output 110 watt
10 ft. by 20 ft.	5	4	3
20 ft. by 20 ft.	8	7	5
20 ft. by 30 ft.	12	9	8
30 ft. by 30 ft.	17	13	11
30 ft. by 50 ft.	29	23	19

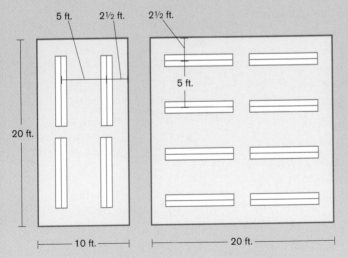

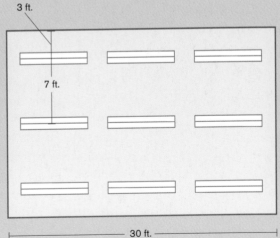

How Many Fixtures Do You Need?

How much light you need depends on the visual difficulty of the work you do and how well your eyes function. Eyesight deteriorates with age, so we need more light as we grow older. Lighting levels are described by a unit of measure called the footcandle (fc). A woodshop should be lit uniformly to a level of 50 fc to 100 fc. You can provide higher levels, if needed, with a separate fixture. Plan for 50 fc if the average worker is less than 40 years of age and doesn't do much work that is difficult to see, such as small, intricate shapes or dark colors. For workers who are more than 40 years of age or who do work that is difficult to see, plan for 100 fc.

As light leaves a fixture and travels to your workbench, it spreads out. You get higher lighting levels near the fixture, with those levels dropping rapidly as the distance from the fixture increases. Because of the diminishing levels of light, you need to limit the maximum spacing between fixtures to avoid dark spots. To figure the maximum spacing between fixtures, you need to know the type of fixtures and the horizontal plane in which visual tasks are performed—for most shops that means the top of the workbench, which is 2½ ft. to 3 ft. off the floor. If fixtures are mounted 10 ft. above the floor and the workbench height is 3 ft., the distance between the fixtures and the workbench is 7 ft.

Typical strip fixtures should have a maximum spacing of 1.6 times that distance, or 11.2 ft. Industrial fixtures should not be spaced more than 1.5 times the distance, or 10.5 ft., for that workspace. Changing the fixture mounting height or the work-plane height will change the maximum spacing. Please note that this recommended spacing is not the optimum; it is the maximum. Closer spacing is usually required to achieve desired lighting levels.

And remember, walls and ceilings should be painted with a flat white paint whenever possible to reflect light more uniformly around the shop.

Another general rule will help to avoid dark shadows where you least want them: The distance from the wall to a row of fixtures should be one-third to one-half the distance between rows of fixtures, because we often locate equipment and workbenches along walls. See the drawings and the chart on p. 165 for more on determining how many fixtures you'll need for a workspace and where to put them. The calculated number of fixtures is seldom a perfect match to the layout of a space, so some juggling may be necessary to fit the fixtures into the room. Don't be afraid to look at alternate layouts before settling on a plan.

Shedding Some Light on Lamps

Fluorescent lamps (see the facing page) are best for lighting small shops. The 8-ft. slimline lamp and the 4-ft. F40 are the most common. Both of these lamps are T12 lamps, meaning the thickness is described in eighths of an inch: 12/8 in., or 1½ in. dia. High-output lamps can be used when higher lighting levels are desired. Smaller T8 (1 in. dia.) lamps are widely used for commercial and industrial lighting, but availability is largely limited to 4-ft. lamps.

Fluorescent lamps are sensitive to ambient temperature, especially when first turned on, and most lamps are produced in two versions—full wattage and energy saving. All full-wattage lamps start reliably at 50°F or higher when operated on standard magnetic ballasts, and 0°F when operated on low-temperature ballasts. Full-wattage high-output lamps will start as low as –20°F on standard ballasts. All energy-saving lamps are rated to start at temperatures of 60°F or higher regardless of the ballast

Lamps

The variety of fluorescent lamps to choose from can make the uninitiated consumer dizzy. Full-wattage 8-ft. slimline lamps draw 75 watts, and the 4-ft. F40s consume 40 watts. Their energy-saving counterparts (labeled by manufacturers with such names as Watt-miser®, Supersaver® and Econ-o-watt®) are rated at 60 watts and 34 watts, respectively. Full-wattage high-output 8-ft. lamps use 110 watts; the 4-ft. versions use 60 watts. To complicate matters more, T12 lamps come with three different styles of bases that must be fitted to matching fixtures.

MATCH THE LAMP BASE TO THE FIXTURE. Fluorescent lamps in all sizes come with a variety of bases to choose from (clockwise from the top): bi-pin, single pin, and recessed double contact.

4-FT. LAMPS   **8-FT. LAMPS**

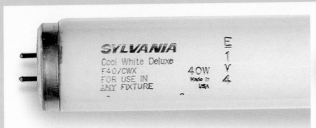 

FULL WATTAGE

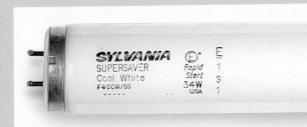 

ENERGY SAVING

HIGH OUTPUT

Ballasts

When you buy a fluorescent light fixture, you're paying mostly for the ballast. Magnetic ballasts are less expensive and more common. With magnetic ballasts, you want to ask for a commercial-grade product. Electronic ballasts weigh less and cost about twice as much. All ballasts make noise—some more than others—and they're all rated on the label to indicate how much noise they make. An "A" rating is the quietest. Be certain the specifications on the ballasts match the size and number of the lamps you want to use in the fixture.

RATING NOISE

The label shown indicates a sound rating of "C," which means that it emits a clearly audible humming noise.

Class P, Type HL
Type 1 Outdoor
High Power Factor
Sound Rated C
Series Ballast
NO PCB's

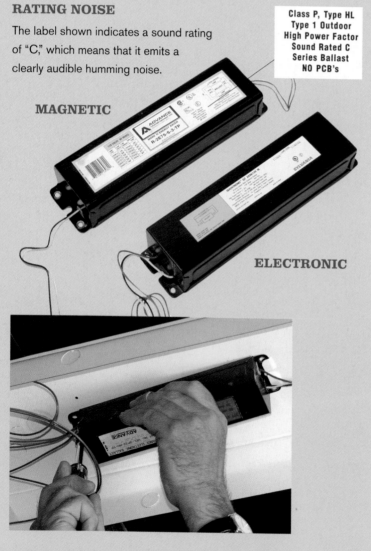

MAGNETIC

ELECTRONIC

SOME NOISE IS FIXABLE. Most ballasts slip into a tab on one end and are fastened with a sheet metal screw into the fixture on the other end. A loose fitting at either location can cause noisy vibrations. Bend the tab or tighten the screw to cure the problem.

type. Contrary to what the names seem to imply, full-wattage lamps are actually more energy efficient than their energy-saving counterparts, which save energy by burning less brightly, not by being more efficient. To understand why, a little history may help.

The National Energy Policy Act of 1992 banned the sale of low-cost, full-wattage lamps in most standard colors, such as cool white and warm white, and required that we buy more expensive energy-saving lamps. This was done as an energy-conservation measure, but it created starting problems in cold-climate areas. As a result, full-wattage cool-white F40 and 8-ft. high-output lamps have been reintroduced in some areas of the country as cold- or low-temperature lamps. Unfortunately, full-wattage cool-white 8-ft. slimline lamps are not available in cold-temperature versions. The only 8-ft. full-wattage slimline lamps available are the high–color rendering types exempted from the Energy Policy Act because of their superior color and premium prices. For example, energy-saving cool-white slimline lamps are available for less than $2 each in case quantities at discount stores such as Costco®. Full-wattage, high–color rendering lamps are typically priced at $7 to $9 each.

In moderate climates, where temperatures at ceiling level are 60°F or higher, energy-saving lamps are preferred because they're cheaper. But if temperatures are normally lower than that, consider heating the shop before turning on the lights. Otherwise, you'll have to use the expensive full-wattage, high–color rendering slimline lamps, cold-temperature high-output lamps, or cold-temperature 4-ft. F40s. The drawback to 4-ft. lamps is that twice as many lamps and fixtures are required to light the space, which increases the labor required to install the system.

Clean Lights Are More Efficient

A little routine maintenance goes a long way toward maximizing the performance of your lighting system. Fixtures and lamps collect dirt and dust, even in the cleanest of shops. A good dust collector and a ceiling-mounted dust filter can't capture all of the dust from woodworking equipment. Dust and dirt on lamps and fixtures can reduce light output by 10 percent or more during the first year, with additional losses of 5 percent or more each year after that. You should clean fixtures and lamps at least once a year to recover this loss. First turn off the power to the fixture. Then remove the lamps, and wash both the lamps and the fixture with a mild solution of water and dishwashing detergent. Rinse with a damp cloth, and dry the surfaces with another clean cloth, or let them air-dry before turning on the power again.

CLEAN LAMPS SHINE BRIGHTER. Dust reduces the light output of fluorescent lamps. Clean them at least annually with a damp cloth and dishwashing detergent.

LET THERE BE LIGHT WHERE IT'S NEEDED. Even though Lindsey chose a uniformly lit approach for his own shop, he had to fill in some areas with task lighting.

Lamps are rated for color Fluorescent lamps come in many different colors and prices. Cool white is the most common and is usually the least expensive, and it has a fair color rendering. If you have to use full-wattage slimline lamps because of temperature constraints, consider the high–color rendering type. GE® calls these lamps SP, Osram®-Sylvania® uses the Designer designation, and Philips® calls them Ultralume. A numeric suffix describes the visual perception of the warmth or coolness of the lighted space: 3,000 is warm, 3,500 is neutral, and 4,100 is cool. Full-wattage deluxe color lamps (such as Cool White Deluxe) are cheaper than high-color rendering lamps, but they are not the best choice for lighting a workshop because they're 25 percent to 33 percent less efficient.

If color matching is important in your work, you can buy special Chroma 50 lamps made specifically for this task. But because they are very expensive and less energy efficient, I would restrict their use to an area where color matching is done.

Weighing in on Ballasts

Fluorescent lamps require a ballast to operate. The ballast provides the high voltage needed to start the lamp and the lower voltage required for normal operation. Ballasts are either magnetic or electronic, with magnetic being more common.

Magnetic ballasts used in fixtures designed for commercial and upper-end residential applications are commercial-grade, transformer types. Almost all 8-ft. fixtures employ this type of ballast. Many 4-ft. fixtures use commercial-grade ballasts, but others contain less expensive residential grades. The commercial versions drive lamps at about 95 percent of their rated light output. They also contain a capacitor to reduce the amount of current drawn by the ballast and can be identified by their larger size and the letters CBM (certified

ballast manufacturer) inside a diamond shape on the label. Residential-grade ballasts produce lower light output, shorten lamp life, and draw more current—all good reasons not to use them.

Some of the 4-ft. shop lights that sell for less than $10 at many retail outlets contain an inexpensive electronic ballast that does not meet the industry standards for commercial ballasts, meaning that lamp life and light output may suffer. Commercial-grade electronic ballasts regulate voltage and current quietly and efficiently, and they seldom produce audible noise.

Magnetic ballasts hum. The bigger the lamp, the more noise the ballast will make. Some hum more than others, and cold temperatures exacerbate the problem. All ballasts have a noise rating printed on the label—an "A" rating is the quietest. Although ballasts can be very noisy when they are started in a cold shop, they should be significantly quieter after they warm up. If you hear excessive noise from one or more fixtures, the cause may be a loose mechanical connection between the ballast and the fixture. Most ballasts are installed with one end slipped into mounting tabs and a screw securing the other end. Make sure the tabs and the screw are tight; if not, tighten the connection. If you still find that one ballast is much noisier than the others, replace it. And if the low-level hum that is typical of fluorescent fixtures in a normal operating mode annoys you, consider masking the noise with a fan, a dust filter, or a radio.

JACK L. LINDSEY retired to the mountains of Oregon in 1996 after a long career as an engineer for the Southern California Edison Co. specializing in commercial and industrial lighting.

Small-Shop Dust Collectors

BY SANDOR
NAGYSZALANCZY

Even woodworkers with no natural housekeeping skills eventually may recognize that the sawdust piling up on the shop floor is a nuisance. Sawdust is also a fire hazard and, worse, poses serious health risks. Some of the bits of dust pumped into the air are many times smaller than the human eye can detect. Dust particles that small can stay aloft for hours, plenty of time to be inhaled and lodge in the deepest cavities of your lungs. Exposure to dust over long periods of time may even give you cancer.

These are good reasons to have a central dust-collection system. A well-designed system whisks wood dust and debris from the machinery, work stations, and floor sweeps to a canister or bag. Good-quality filters capture most of the dust before the air is returned to the shop. Any small particles that sneak through can be controlled with an air-filtration device or by wearing a dust mask. The result is a healthier and cleaner shop.

You can get good results by mounting a collector on a dolly and wheeling it from job to job. But I think a central collection system—consisting of a collector, rigid metal ducts, and flexible hose—is the best approach. A good central collector is tailored to suit the equipment in your shop.

Central Collectors vs. Shop Vacuums

Shop vacuums or small portable collectors work well when collecting dust from a single machine or from portable power tools. But many of them don't have much chip-holding capacity. A shop vacuum has a small universal motor, like those that are used in most portable power tools, running at a high speed to drive a fan that draws sawdust through a 1-in. to 2¼-in. flexible hose. Hoses that small can clog easily with large shavings.

A central collector is like a big shop-vacuum cleaner, with some important differences. A central collector employs a powerful induction motor (the kind used in most stationary machines) to drive a large-volume fan. This blower, or impeller, moves chips and sawdust through ductwork 3 in. to 6 in. or more in diameter. A central dust collector moves a large volume of air at 3,500 to 4,000 feet per minute (fpm)—a speed just high enough to keep chips and dust moving through the ducts in a well-designed system.

In contrast, a shop vacuum moves a small volume of air at a high velocity—8,000 fpm or more—through a small-diameter hose. This high-velocity air is subject to more friction, which is why these machines

CHOOSING A COLLECTOR

SINGLE-STAGE COLLECTORS, such as this 2-hp unit, connect easily to small central-collection systems. One drawback is that the debris enters through the unit's blower, where cutoffs or stray bits of metal can cause problems.

THE LID CAN BE HEAVY with this kind of two-stage collector. One option would be to install a block and tackle nearby with a wall cleat to tie off the rope.

Single-stage collector
With a single-stage collector, all air, fine dust, large chips, and debris are drawn through the blower.

Fabric bags filter fine dust.

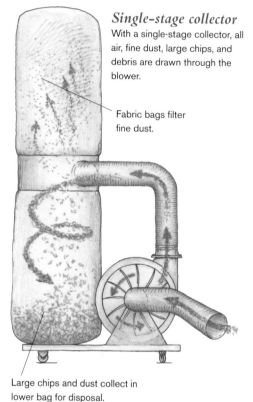

Large chips and dust collect in lower bag for disposal.

Two-stage collector
With a two-stage collector, like the canister style shown here, large chips and debris settle out when air and wood dust enter the canister.

Only fine dust passes through the blower and into the filter bag.

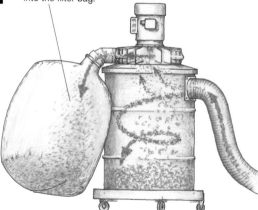

quickly choke if you try to draw sawdust through more than just a few feet of hose.

Two-Stage Systems Are Safer and More Efficient

Once you've decided to buy a central dust collector for your shop, you are faced with a number of choices. The most basic is whether to go with a single-stage or a two-stage design (see the drawings at left). Prices range from less than $200 for a 1-hp single-stage version to more than $2,500 for a big-capacity two-stage collector.

Single-stage collectors are widely advertised in woodworking-supply catalogs and magazines, and most of them are manufactured in Taiwan. These simple devices consist of a blower and a filter-bag assembly (see the top photo at left). Incoming dust and chips travel through the blower and then into fabric bags. The lower bag collects the sawdust.

A two-stage collector removes larger particles and coarse dust before air enters the blower. Most two-stage collectors use either a canister or a cyclone (more about cyclones later) to separate heavier debris. Only fine dust moves through the blower and into the filters.

Two-stage collectors have several advantages over single-stage models. Because large debris doesn't go through the blower, there's less wear and tear on the fan and less racket caused by chunks of wood striking the blower. More important, this reduces the risk of a fire or explosion. Bits of metal, like a nail or a staple, can cause a spark when they hit the blower and ignite dust inside the filter bag. When only very fine dust is sent to the filters, they become more efficient: The filters are less likely to clog, they will need to be cleaned less often, and they will allow air to flow more freely through the system.

Disadvantages? Canister-style collectors and cyclone collectors are more expensive than comparably sized single-stage units, and many two-stage systems are just too big for small shops.

One drawback to canister-style collectors, sometimes called barrel-top collectors, is that you must lift off a heavy top assembly to empty the drum (see the bottom photo on the facing page). You can make that chore easier by hooking a block and tackle to a ceiling joist over the unit to raise and lower the top.

The low cost and availability of single-stage models make them popular in many small woodworking shops. With a pre-separator added in front of the blower, a single-stage collector will perform like a two-stage unit. This conversion will increase the chip-holding capacity of the collector and make sawdust easier to empty. More important, it will allow you to collect larger chips and metal debris more safely.

Cyclones, Separator Cans, and Drop Boxes

A cyclone is one kind of pre-separator. It's a sheet-metal cylinder with a funnel-shaped lower section that empties into a drum. Incoming air full of dust and chips swirls around until the heavier debris slows down and drops to the bottom.

You can purchase a system with a built-in cyclone, such as the Delta 50-900 series (see the top photo on p. 176). Or you can build or buy a cyclone and connect it to a single-stage system. Be sure the cyclone fits the air-moving capacity of your blower and ductwork system.

If you can't afford a cyclone, you can add a pre-separator to your system by installing either a dust-separator can or a drop box ahead of the blower. Though they are less efficient than a cyclone, these devices are inexpensive and can increase the chip-holding capacity of your system.

A dust-separator can is a drum or a barrel with an inlet and an outlet arranged so that heavier materials settle out as dust

and debris enter it. Only fine dust travels to the blower and the filters.

You can build your own separator can by installing a few plastic plumbing fittings into the removable lid of a fiber or steel drum. Flexible hoses connect the inlet to the ductwork and the exhaust to the blower. Or you can buy a cast-plastic lid that's designed to fit over a standard 30-gal. galvanized-steel trash can (see the bottom photo on p. 176). This inexpensive lid accepts 4-in.-dia. hoses and hooks up quickly to most systems. The lid is available through a number of woodworking-supply catalogs.

A drop box is an even more basic pre-separator (see the drawing on p. 177). It consists of an airtight plywood box with an inside baffle. As air from the ductwork enters on one side, chips settle and fall into a removable bin inside the box.

Choose a Collector with Enough Power

To determine the size and power of a central collector, you'll need to know two things: the amount of air the collector's blower is capable of moving, measured in cubic feet per minute (cfm) and the amount of air resistance in the ductwork that the collector must overcome, stated as static pressure (sp). Generally, more motor horsepower and larger blowers mean more air-moving capacity for the collection system. The amount of power you'll need depends on three factors:

1. How much sawdust your shop produces. The more debris a machine produces, the greater the volume of air needed to capture and convey it. See the chart on p. 178 for average cfm requirements for small-shop machines.

2. How far the ductwork must move sawdust. The farther or more roundabout the distance debris must travel, the stronger the collector you'll need. Ribbed, flexible hose generates more friction than straight,

A BUILT-IN CYCLONE does an excellent job separating chips and dust before they reach the blower. This Delta 50-903 collector has a 5-hp motor.

A CHEAPER ALTERNATIVE This cast-plastic separator lid (with a 1½-hp Penn State #DC3 portable collector) fits snugly on a 30-gal. trash can. Connected to a ductwork system, the lid isolates large debris and transforms a single-stage collector into a safer two-stage unit.

smooth-walled duct. Small-diameter ducts add more friction and require more power.

3. How many machines the collection system must handle simultaneously. In most ductwork systems, blast gates control the suction at each work station. Running several machines at once with two or three gates open, common in a shop with several people, requires more air and power than running a single machine with only one gate open.

If your shop is about the size of a two-car garage and you use only one machine at a time, your central collector should deliver at least 5 in. of sp and about 20 percent-50 percent more cfm than is required by your largest dust-producing machine, as shown in the chart on p. 178. Use a 4-in. pipe for most branch ducts; thickness planers need a 5-in. pipe. Connect the branches to a 5-in.-dia. or 6-in.-dia. main duct.

If your shop is larger or your collection system is more complicated, the only way to ensure you'll end up with the right size central collector is to design your entire system first. This involves laying out and sizing all the system's main and branch ducts, figuring the cfm needs for all the machines used at one time, and calculating the air resistance, or sp losses, in the system.

This process is too complicated to cover in this chapter, but if you are up to doing the calculations yourself, Air Handling Systems (5 Lunar Drive, Woodbridge, CT 06525; 800-367-3828) offers a free catalog with instructions for doing the math. The company also sells a simple calculator, which works like a slide rule.

If you need more help in designing your system, your local air-handling equipment supplier usually can help. Oneida Air Systems (1001 W. Fayette St., Syracuse, NY 13204; 315-476-5151) is one dealer that provides free design services.

Advertised vs. actual performance Be aware that the cfm ratings you see in some

advertisements reflect the amount of air a collector moves when it's not connected to any ductwork and is operating with no resistance (that's 0 sp). This is known as free-air cfm. Static-pressure ratings also can be misleading because they can represent the pressure loss generated when no air is moving at all, or at 0 cfm.

So how do you really know how much power a collector is capable of generating at a particular cfm? You can ask the manufacturer for a copy of the collector's performance curve. (The performance curve is a graph that plots the actual amount of air the collector will convey under different work loads.) If the dealer can't supply you with one, I suggest buying a unit from one who can, or select a model that is sized at least 50 percent larger than your requirements.

What If Your Collector Isn't Strong Enough?

If you own an underpowered collector, you'll know by the telltale sawdust that accumulates around your equipment. Chips that have settled in the ductwork are another sure sign. If you can't afford to buy a new one, there are a few things that you can do to improve the efficiency of your present collector:

1. Relocate the collector so that it's closer to the machines and floor sweeps. When you reduce the length of ductwork and straighten the number of twists and turns, you lower the resistance to air flow.

2. If dust collection is inadequate at only one machine, such as the planer, move it closer to the blower. Or you could disconnect it from your main system and use a separate dedicated collector to service just that machine.

3. Add more power by connecting two dust collectors in tandem. You'll nearly double the force of your system by attaching two units together. Run a hose from the outlet of one blower to the inlet

of another. To avoid pressure imbalances, use two identical units.

4. Buy a larger dust bag, or retrofit the fan-inlet plate with a larger duct (both are available from Oneida Air Systems). These methods work especially well with many single-stage collectors. Just like fitting bigger carburetors or mufflers to an auto engine, these new components help the unit convey a larger volume of air. Oneida Air Systems also sells large replacement bags.

Getting Good Filtration

Exhaust from the blower must pass through a filter to remove fine dust and return clean air to the shop. The quality of filtration depends on the kind of fabric material used and the filter's total surface area.

Good and better filter materials If you purchased a single-stage collector a few years ago, it probably came with a cotton sateen or a cotton duck fabric bag. These do a poor job of filtering out dust particles smaller than 30 microns (1 micron is a millionth of a meter).

Dust particles below 10 microns do the most respiratory damage. Most of the collectors sold today come with bags sewn from polyester fabrics—they're better at filtering out harmful dust. Some manufacturers offer them as an alternative to cheaper cotton bags.

Polyester fibers can be woven, knitted, or felted (see the photo on p. 178). Filter bags that are made from 12-oz. or 16-oz. felted polyester, singed on the inside by a gas flame to keep the fabric from becoming clogged, are very popular for general woodworking. They can capture 99.5 percent of very fine dust particles between 0.2 and 2 microns. For advice on which fabric is best for your collector, consult with a filter-bag company, such as Midwesco Filter Resources (400 Battaile Drive, Winchester, VA 22601; 800-336-7300).

A DROP BOX CREATES A TWO-STAGE SYSTEM FROM A SINGLE-STAGE COLLECTOR

This 36-in. by 60-in. box, built from ¾-in. plywood, is about right for a system that moves 1,000 cfm. The size of the box is not critical, as long as you make it airtight.

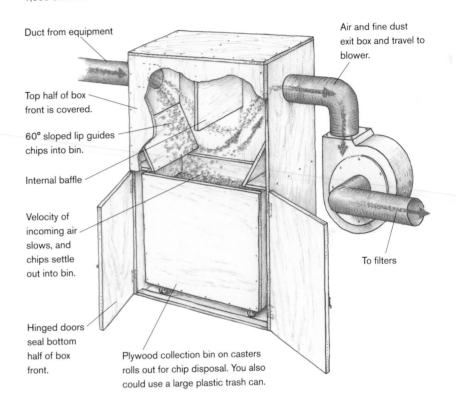

Duct from equipment

Air and fine dust exit box and travel to blower.

Top half of box front is covered.

60° sloped lip guides chips into bin.

Internal baffle

Velocity of incoming air slows, and chips settle out into bin.

To filters

Hinged doors seal bottom half of box front.

Plywood collection bin on casters rolls out for chip disposal. You also could use a large plastic trash can.

Dust cake and filter cleaning Fine dust builds up quickly on the inside surface of a filter, forming a film that's known as dust cake. In one way, this is good because the cake acts as a filter in its own right—the buildup of particles blocks the passage of finer and finer dust.

But as a filter becomes more clogged (industry pamphlets call this "blinded"), the air passing through the bag has more difficulty escaping. The mounting static pressure inside the bag actually reduces air flow through the entire collection system. Excess pressure will eventually force fine particles right through the fabric. To keep dust cake from getting too thick, shake the bags occasionally.

Getting enough filter surface area No amount of cleaning will keep a filter bag working efficiently if there isn't enough

The Kinds of Fabrics Matter

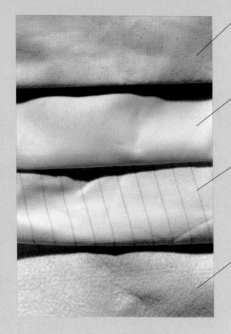

COTTON SATEEN is the least expensive and the least effective at filtering fine dust. It's also more prone to rot and mildew.

WOVEN POLYESTER is more durable but not much better at capturing fine dust.

KNITTED POLYESTER stretches like the material used to make athletic tube socks. It's thick enough for good filtration. The dark lines in this bag are carbon fibers, which help dissipate static electricity.

FELTED POLYESTER has no nap (like wool felt) and tends to be more expensive than woven polyester. Its thickness creates a three-dimensional maze that traps fine dust particles better than all the other samples shown.

surface area. An air-to-cloth ratio is the comparison of a collector's cfm rating to the total square-foot area of its filters.

For general woodworking, an air-to-cloth ratio of 10:1 is about right. So for every 10 cfm of air delivered, you will need 1 sq. ft. of filter area. Many small-shop dust collectors are skimpy on filter area. It is not uncommon to find single-stage units with air-to-cloth ratios of 35:1 or more. On many models, the lower bag also serves as a dust bin, which further reduces the effective filter area.

In addition to replacing original bags with larger ones, you can gain even more filter-surface area by building a plenum that directs exhaust from the blower to multiple filter bags, or tubes. By using small-diameter tubes, you can add a surprising amount of filter area in a few square feet of shop space. And clean air makes a more enjoyable workplace.

SANDOR NAGYSZALANCZY is a writer and contributing editor to *Fine Woodworking* magazine.

AIR VOLUME REQUIRED FOR SMALL-SHOP WOODWORKING MACHINES

Machine	Average cfm needed
Tablesaw (8 in. to 12 in.)	350–500
Bandsaw (up to 15 in.)	400
Radial-arm saw (10 in. to 12 in.)	400
Scrollsaw	350
Jointer (up to 8 in.)	400
Planer (up to 12 in.)	500
Shaper (½-in. to ¾-in. arbor)	350–450
Lathe	450
Disk (12 in.) or belt sander (6 in.)	400

Note: These numbers are averages based on duct sizes of 4 in. or 5 in. dia. A shaper cutting a crown molding needs more air volume than the same machine trimming a bevel on a shelf edge. Call the manufacturer or an air-handling equipment supplier for exact figures.
cfm = cubic feet per minute.

Dust Collection for the One-Man Shop

BY ANATOLE BURKIN

Don't throw away the broom just yet. Even the best dust-collection system won't eliminate the need for occasional sweeping. A good system, however, will keep the broom and your lungs from wearing out prematurely.

There are two main points to consider when choosing a dust collector. First, figure out the air-volume requirements of the machines in your shop (see the chart on p. 182). Next, decide on what kind of hookups you are going to use: flexible hose, PVC pipe, or metal duct.

To see what size and type of collector would best suit a one-man shop, I gathered a sampling of machines, from 1-hp single-stage units to 2-hp two-stage collectors, including one cyclone: Delta® (1½ hp single stage), Dust Boy (2 hp two stage), Jet® (2 hp single stage), Oneida (1½ hp cyclone), and SECO® UFO-90 (1 hp single stage). I used the collectors with my tools, which include a 10-in. cabinet saw, a 15-in. planer, an 8-in. jointer, and a 16-in. bandsaw.

The horsepower rating is a fairly reliable guide to the performance of a dust collector (see the chart on p. 183). Hookups, however, are everything. Too much flexible hose will rob even a big collector of power. PVC pipes, in short runs, work fine with a sufficiently

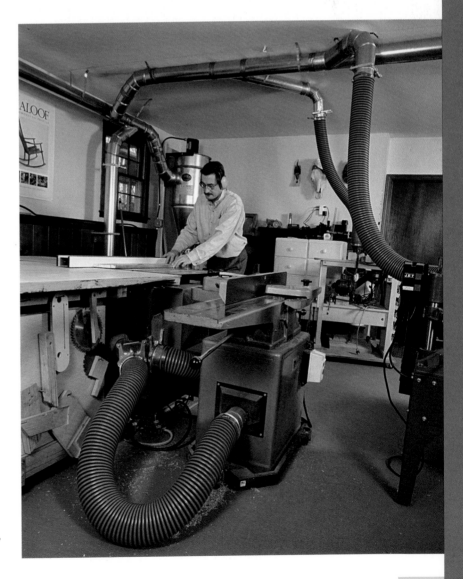

Three Styles of Dust Collectors

The most economical and biggest-selling dust collectors are the two-bag, single-stage models. Single stage means the dust is sucked through the impeller (fan) and dumped into the lower bag. The upper bag collects fine sawdust and lets the exhaust air back into the shop.

Two-stage collectors are the next step up. The motor and impeller sit atop a barrel. Chips enter the barrel and are directed downward, although the swirling air inside may occasionally move smaller chips upward. A filter bag hangs off to one side and collects the finest dust.

Two-stage cyclones are at the top of the evolutionary chain. The motor and impeller sit atop a cone-shaped canister, the cyclone, which is connected to a trash can below. Chips or other large debris enter the cyclone and swirl downward, avoiding the impeller. The longer the cyclonic chamber, the greater its effectiveness at slowing down and separating large particles. Air is filtered either by a pleated internal cartridge or by one or more felt bags hanging off to the side of the machine. Internal-cartridge cyclones use the least amount of floor space. The upper bags or cartridge filters of all collectors must be shaken out occasionally to remove fine dust.

DANGERS OF SINGLE-STAGE COLLECTORS

Debris entering a single-stage collector passes through the impeller, many of which are made of steel. Even a small bit of metal, such as a screw, can cause a spark when it hits a steel impeller. Dust-collector explosions are rare, but the potential is there. Debris, metal or otherwise, not only makes a racket when it hits an impeller but also imparts stress on the bearing and will shorten its life. I heard of a woodworker whose collector's sheet-metal housing was punctured by a screw that entered the impeller.

One way to reduce the risk of fire is to choose a single-stage collector with a plastic or aluminum impeller. Although the impeller itself won't cause a spark, metal debris striking the steel housing may have the same effect. Steel impellers are fine, however, if you avoid using the dust collector to sweep up miscellaneous debris off the floor or workbench.

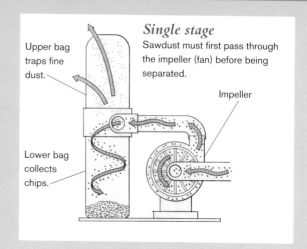

Single stage
Sawdust must first pass through the impeller (fan) before being separated.

Upper bag traps fine dust.

Impeller

Lower bag collects chips.

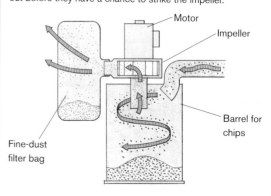

Barrel-style two stage
The larger chips entering a two-stage collector tend to drop out before they have a chance to strike the impeller.

Motor

Impeller

Fine-dust filter bag

Barrel for chips

Two-stage cyclone
The shape of a cyclone is most efficient at slowing down the speed of debris, allowing most of it to settle out before reaching the filter.

Motor

Impeller

Internal filter for fine dust

Cyclonic chamber

Barrel for chips

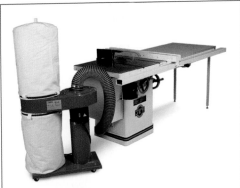

1-HP COLLECTORS Small, portable collectors are easy to move around the shop. Make connections to one tool at a time using a short piece of flexible hose.

powered collector, 1½ hp or more. Metal duct, not unexpectedly, performs best. Even an 8-year-old, 1-hp collector can collect chips from machines 25 ft. away when hooked up to a properly designed system. Using a 1-hp collector this way may seem misguided, like putting a racing exhaust system on a subcompact car, but "the experiment illustrates how you don't have to spend a fortune to get decent results. Every shop is different, of course, and your results may vary, so use my findings as guidelines, not absolutes.

A 1-hp Single-Stage Collector Can Handle Any Machine in My Shop

The biggest sawdust producer in my shop is a 15-in. planer. And even a 1-hp single-stage dust collector can handle that machine, hooked up with about 6 ft. of 4-in.-dia. flexible hose. I borrowed a new UFO-90, same as my old collector, to see if anything had been changed. It's still the same machine, rated at 650 cu. ft. per minute (cfm) by the manufacturer, but when hooked up to 6 ft. of flexible hose, it moves about 420 cfm. That's slightly less than the 500 cfm recommended for a 15-in. planer, but 90 percent of the time the 1-hp collector can handle it because I rarely plane 15-in.-wide stock.

One-hp single-stage collectors cost about $200. Some woodworkers buy two units and station them strategically in their

shop. At 82 decibels (measured at 8 ft.), a 1-hp dust collector isn't much noisier than a vacuum cleaner, and each one takes up about 3 sq. ft. of shop space.

I also used the 1-hp collector with a PVC duct system (4-in.-dia. pipe and fittings) and measured the moving air volume at the tablesaw-jointer connection, which is at the end of about 25 ft. of pipe and hose. At that distance, because of increased resistance, the air volume drops to under 300 cfm, less than recommended for woodworking tools. In reality, however, one can live with that. But if I'm face-jointing wide boards, the collector can't always handle the volume, and chips jam the jointer's dust port. Maybe 80 percent of the time it works okay.

When I hooked up the 1-hp collector to a newly installed metal duct system, with my tools in the same configuration as before, I was really surprised. The air volume was back up to 360 cfm, very acceptable. Then I hooked up my old 1-hp collector, which is outfitted with oversized felt bags (available from Oneida Air Systems) that improve airflow and capture fine dust (see the sidebar on p. 184), and I measured almost 400 cfm. That's a significant gain.

1½-HP COLLECTORS Although collectors in this power category may occasionally be used with two tools simultaneously, for best performance, use blast gates and run one tool at a time.

MAKING SENSE OF MANUFACTURER SPECS

There's a fair amount of misleading marketing specs on dust collectors. When an ad says a collector is rated at 1,200 cfm, what does it mean? Not much, really. Cfm stands for cubic feet per minute, a measure of the volume of air moving past a point of reference. The cfm figure needs to be put in the context of the amount of resistance, or friction, present (called static pressure, or sp). Air moving through duct or hose encounters resistance, just as a person would slipping down a water slide. The more bends and bumps, the slower the ride or the lower the air velocity and volume. Many manufacturers rate their machines without bags or duct attached.

While trying out a number of dust collectors, I measured their performances under real working conditions, using flexible hose, PVC pipe, or metal duct in my 420-sq.-ft. shop (see the chart on the facing page). The resistance readings ranged from 3 in. to 5 in. I also measured collectors hooked up to a straight piece of 6-in.-dia. metal duct, just to get a baseline, highest-possible performance figure.

Collectors ranging in size from 1 hp to 2 hp have impellers (fans) sized from 10 in. dia. to 12 in. dia. All things being equal (motor speed and impeller design), a bigger impeller coupled with a bigger motor will move more air than a smaller pairing. There are some differences among collectors; to learn more, ask a manufacturer for an impeller performance chart.

As soon as any collector is hooked up in the shop, performance declines in relation to the length and type of hookup. That's why smooth-walled metal duct, with wide-radius elbows and wyes, is better than PVC pipe.

AIR-VOLUME REQUIREMENTS OF MACHINES

Tool	cfm needed
10-in. tablesaw	350
6-in. or 8-in. jointer	300–450
12-in. planer	350
15-in. planer	500
Drill press	350
14-in. or 16-in. bandsaw	350
Radial-arm saw	350–500
12-in. disc sander	350
12-in. to 24-in. drum sander	300–500
Oscillating spindle sander	350
Floor sweep	350

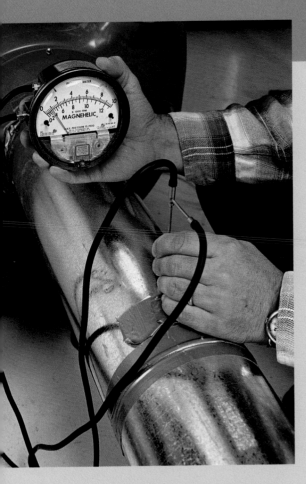

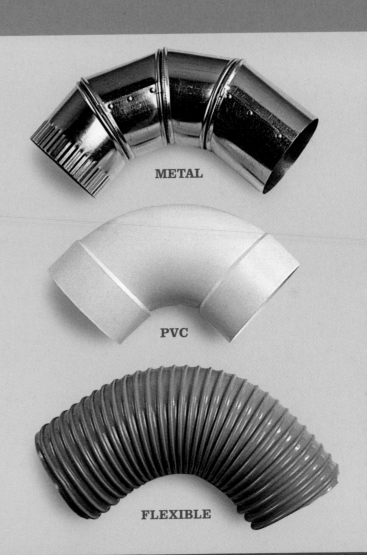

METAL

PVC

FLEXIBLE

MEASUREMENTS WERE TAKEN WITH A DIAL-GAUGE MANOMETER (A PRESSURE GAUGE) AND PITOT TUBE. The chart below compares the performance of a few dust collectors when using hose, PVC pipe, and metal duct.

PERFORMANCE OF DUST COLLECTORS UNDER VARYING CONDITIONS

Horsepower	6 ft. from collector, 6-in.-dia. straight metal duct*	6 ft. from collector, 4-in.-dia. flexible hose	6 ft. from collector, two runs of 4-in.-dia. flexible hose	25 ft. from collector, at jointer hookup, 4-in.-dia. PVC pipe	25 ft. from collector, at jointer hookup, 5-in.-dia. metal duct
1 hp single stage	550 cfm	Excellent	Fair	Fair	Excellent
1½ hp single stage	825 cfm	Excellent	Good	Good	Excellent
1½ hp cyclone	700 cfm	Excellent	Good	Good	Excellent
2 hp single stage	980 cfm	Excellent	Excellent	Excellent	Excellent
2 hp two stage	825 cfm	Excellent	Good	Good	Excellent

Fair: under 300 cfm   Good: 325 cfm to 350 cfm   Excellent: more than 350 cfm
* Bags or filters attached with a light coating of sawdust present.

Go with Felt Bags

The standard bags issued with most dust collectors are good for capturing particles of 25 to 30 microns or bigger. A micron is 1/1,000,000th of a meter in length; looked at another way, the paper this chapter is printed on is about 25 microns thick. Fine dust blows right through filter fabric, back into the shop. Dust particles under 10 microns in size are the most harmful because they can get past the respiratory tract and enter your lungs. Unless you wear a dust mask while woodworking, toss out the stock bags and replace them with felt bags rated at 5 microns or less.

FABRIC VS. FELT. A fabric bag, left, has less thickness and is more porous. Felt, right, does a much better job of filtering out very fine dust.

A 1½-hp Collector Can Be Hooked up to Longer Runs of Hose or Duct

As you might imagine, hooked up to one machine at a time, a 1½-hp collector does not have any trouble removing chips, even with a long (12-ft.) run of hose. Delta rates its 1½-hp collector at 1,200 cfm, a number that is derived in a lab, not under real shop conditions. Hooked up to a 6-ft. run of 4-in.-dia. flexible hose, I measured about 500 cfm with the Delta and 470 cfm using an Oneida Air Systems 1½-hp cyclone collector. Cyclones and two-stage collectors have slightly more internal air resistance; hence the lower cfm reading. That's about what you can expect from any 1½-hp collector hooked up to 4-in.-dia. hose.

I also hooked up the 1½-hp collectors to two machines running simultaneously. Performance ranged from good to so-so, depending on how much sawdust was being spit out by my tools. The best way to direct maximum airflow to the tool being used is to attach a blast gate to each hose.

Hooked up to a PVC duct system (a run of about 25 ft. of pipe), both the Delta and Oneida collectors captured most of the sawdust when running one tool.

A 1½-hp Delta collector costs about $350. A two-stage unit such as the Oneida costs almost twice as much. Penn State Industries also sells a cyclone collector. (For more on the advantages of two-stage collectors vs. single-stage units, see the sidebar on p. 180.)

Both 1½-hp collectors performed exceptionally well when connected to metal duct and used with one tool at a time. With two blast gates open, the air volume dropped and was insufficient to operate two big machines at once.

The larger-volume bags or canisters of 1½-hp collectors hold a lot of material, about 30 gal. worth, which means fewer trips to the compost pile, a big advantage over the 1-hp machines that hold about half of that. A 1½-hp single-stage collector takes up about 7 sq. ft. of shop space. But a vertically stacked two-stage cyclone such as the Oneida takes up only 3½ sq. ft.

2-HP COLLECTORS

SINGLE STAGE Many 2-hp collectors can handle two tools at once. Although 4-in.-dia. PVC pipe is not the best duct material, satisfactory results can be obtained when connected to a 2-hp collector.

BARREL-STYLE TWO STAGE A 2-hp collector has enough power to handle larger machinery, such as this 18-in. planer (right). This collector by Dust Boy is a two-stage model with a 55-gal. drum.

of shop space, a big plus in a small shop. More horsepower does mean more noise; both registered 85 decibels at 8 ft. The Delta comes wired for 115 volts but can be switched over to 230 volts. The Oneida comes without cable or switch. It can be wired to run on either current.

A 2-hp Unit Can Sometimes Handle Two Machines at Once

Hooked up to two 6-ft. runs of 4-in.-dia. hoses, a 2-hp single-stage collector draws over 350 cfm from each port, plenty for many woodworking machines. The 2-hp two-stage Dust Boy didn't match the power of the 2-hp single-stage Jet machine, although it has other qualities that may be preferable. When I connected the 2-hp units to the PVC duct system, they too were robbed of considerable power, but one machine could be operated at a time with satisfactory results.

When connected to a metal duct system, the Jet collector really moved a lot of air, 570 cfm at the tablesaw-jointer connection (after about 25 ft. of duct). With two blast

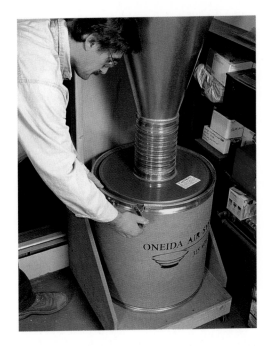

BETTER CONNECTIONS. The Oneida cyclone collector's trash barrel is connected by a large metal ring, which simplifies reattachment (left). Woodworker's Supply sells a clamp-on skirt accessory that is used with a 30-gal. trash can (right). The skirt is easier to reattach than a standard lower bag.

Sources of Supply

Air Handling Systems
800-367-3828
Duct supplies and duct design

American Fabric Filter Co.
800-367-3591
Custom-made dust bags

Delta
800-438-2486
Dust collectors

Highland Hardware
800-241-6748
Dust collectors

Kraemer Tools
800-443-6443
Dust collectors and supplies (Canada)

Nordfab
800-532-0830
Quick-Fit duct supplies

Oneida Air Systems
315-476-5151
Dust collectors, duct supplies and duct design

Penn State Industries
800-377-7297
Dust collectors and supplies

Sunhill Machinery
800-929-4321
Dust collectors and supplies

Woodworker's Supply
800-645-9292
Dust collectors and supplies

Wilke Machinery
800-235-2100
Dust collectors and supplies

gates open, the air volume was reduced to less than 300 cfm, still acceptable for some operations. The Dust Boy produced slightly lower readings but still had more than enough power to run one tool at a time in any configuration. If you regularly operate more than one machine simultaneously, it would be wise to look at 3-hp or bigger dust collectors.

The 2-hp machines are no noisier than the 1½-hp collectors. They cost more, however. The Jet is priced at $400; the Dust Boy sells for about $650. Most 2-hp collectors come wired for 230 volts. The Dust Boy can be run at either 115 volts or 230 volts.

Choosing among the Options

On the matter of choosing a dust collector, a two-stage cyclone gets my top vote. A small cyclone collector takes up less room, is easy to empty, and runs very clean. For example, on all of the single-stage units, even after running them for only an hour, fine dust appeared on the machine and in the area around it. That's because it's difficult to get a perfect seal between the bag and housing. The Oneida cyclone, outfitted with an internal filter, rubber gaskets, and wide metal ring clamps, seals better.

Two-stage units such as the Dust Boy (Delta also makes a two-stage collector) are also nice and compact. The Dust Boy takes up 6 sq. ft. and less vertical space than most collectors. The Dust Boy (as does the Oneida) comes with a Leeson® motor and cast-aluminum housing and impeller (fan), and the sturdy plastic barrel holds a lot of debris, 55 gal. worth. Before it can be emptied, however, the heavy motor and housing must be lifted off.

Removing the lower bag of a single-stage collector is an easy matter of loosening a band clamp. The real fun begins when you try to reattach it. If you've ever had to put your pants on with an arm in a cast, you'll get the idea. The lower bag must

be wrapped around the metal waist of the machine and held in place before the clamp can be cinched. Some manufacturers, such as Jet, add an elastic band inside the lower bag to facilitate reattachment somewhat.

Woodworker's Supply tried to solve the lower-bag problem with a clamp-on skirt accessory. The skirt and a standard 30-gal. trash can replace the lower bag. Because the skirt remains attached to the collector's housing, it's easy to cinch the lower belt that attaches the skirt to the trash can. I just wish the skirt were made of felt rather than the more porous woven fabric. This setup will reduce the air volume (the collector "breathes" through both bags) when using the stock upper bag. With a larger upper bag, I found that the cfm readings were not compromised. But if you happen to vacuum up any offcuts, they will make quite a racket rattling around in a metal trash can.

Although many woodworkers, myself included, have used PVC drainpipe for duct without mishap, experts warn against using the material. The connectors (elbows and wyes) restrict airflow, and the material builds up a static charge, which may cause a spark and set off an explosion. (Running grounded copper wire inside the pipe reduces the hazard.) Use PVC at your own risk. Metal duct and fittings are obviously better and will also last longer. I've broken half a dozen plastic blast gates in as many years. If you're on a tight budget, go with flexible hose or build a metal duct system in stages, starting with only a couple of hookups. Your collector will work more efficiently, and so will you.

ANATOLE BURKIN is the publisher of *Fine Woodworking* and an avid woodworker.

Designing a Central Dust-Collection System

Oneida Air Systems designed my ductwork, which is very typical for a one-room shop under 500 sq. ft. The ductwork begins with a 6-in.-dia. pipe connected to the collector. At the first wye (split), the duct reduces to 5-in.-dia. branches. The 5-in.-dia. pipes serve the biggest tools (jointer, tablesaw, and planer), even though they all have 4-in.-dia. dust ports, which ensure good air volume to the machines. Also, you can change the dust port to a 5-in.-dia. connection for better performance. A 5-in.-dia. to 4-in.-dia. reducer is used to make the transition.

The 4-in.-dia. branches that split off the 5-in.-dia. line serve smaller tools, such as the bandsaw and router table. Blast gates are installed at each tool. The final connections were made with flexible hose, which allows me to move my tools around.

I used 24-gauge (mostly) snap-lock pipe, spot-welded fittings, and aluminum blast gates, which are available from many companies. (Avoid lighter-gauge metal duct designed for heating or cooling systems; it can collapse under vacuum.)

A higher-quality system will employ 22-gauge spiral pipe and welded fittings, which are stiffer and more airtight, and yes, they cost more. Quick-Fit duct supplies from Nordfab are also premium priced, but the components go together easily and don't require duct tape or caulk.

Although individual 24-gauge components aren't that expensive (a 5-ft. run of 5-in.-dia. snap-lock pipe costs about $8), it all adds up. A very basic three-machine setup may be had for a few hundred dollars. A

system for half a dozen tools and a floor sweep may cost $500 or more.

To help illustrate the photos in this chapter, an orange/black flex hose was used to make connections from pipe to tools; black flex hose, however, works fine. It's best to use a minimum of hose because it produces about three times the friction of metal pipe. Friction will reduce the performance of the system. All pipe seams and connections must be sealed with caulk or duct tape. Clear silicone caulk is a good choice because it's virtually invisible and is easy to remove.

DESIGN HELP IS AVAILABLE

Designing the ductwork for a central dust-collection system can involve a lot of calculations. For those of us who skipped math class, there's help available.

• Air Handling Systems of Woodbridge, Conn., has an on-line duct calculator program (www.airhand.com). The company outlines the concepts of duct design in a four-page brochure.

• Oneida Air Systems of Syracuse, N.Y., will design a duct system free of charge for its customers (www.oneida-air.com). All that's required is a shop drawing showing the types and locations of woodworking machines.

• Nordfab of Thomasville, N.C., manufacturers of the Quick-Fit line of duct and fittings, offers a free design service. The company has a downloadable program (www.nordfab.com), but you need a CAD program to run it. The company also offers a peel-and-stick shop layout kit for analog woodworkers.

Dust Collection Demystified

BY GARRETT HACK

Woodworkers have been battling sawdust ever since the ancients invented the handsaw about 5,000 years ago. The Egyptians cleverly disposed of at least some woodworking debris by using it to stuff mummies, but this is not an option for today's woodworker.

In more recent times, the dust and chips created by woodworking machines has grown vastly more plentiful, finer, and more hazardous. Prolonged exposure can cause respiratory problems and has been linked to the development of some types of cancer. So keeping all of this material out of the air and off your tools and floor, and gathering it for disposal, have become more urgent and more challenging tasks.

Enter the dust collector.

A woodshop dust collector is a simple exhaust system. Its blower moves contaminated air through hose or ductwork to filters, which clean that air for recirculation back into the shop. The more effective the blower, the more ductwork you can add and still have enough suction at the other end to do the job.

For many woodworkers, a shop vacuum is the first dust collector. A shop vac can handle small amounts of fine debris like that produced by a 5-in. orbital sander or a router. But a shop vac moves small volumes of air, making it a poor choice for larger stationary machines.

Dust collectors generally belong to one of two families. Single-stage collectors carry the sawdust and other debris directly through the fan and into filter bags or cartridges. Two-stage cyclone collectors allow heavier debris to drop out of the airstream before it reaches the blower, meaning less work and abuse for the fan and filters.

The more air a dust collector moves, the more debris it can carry. Dust from a small hand sander might be captured effectively with as little as 100 cu. ft. per minute (cfm), but a tablesaw might require 800 cfm. Also, the faster a collector moves the air, the heavier the debris it can carry. The lightweight dust from a small sander might need an airspeed of as little as 3,000 linear ft. per minute (fpm). The coarser material produced by a planer often demands as much as 4,000 fpm. Finally, the more effective a dust collector's filters, the less fine dust will be returned to the air.

Dust-collection systems are like many other things in life: The safest approach is to plan for the worst. Some modestly powered dust collectors can deliver 800 cfm only if connected to a machine by less than 4 ft. of flexible hose. The bigger challenge lies in collecting dust from machines on the far side of the room. A key question to consider about any dust collector is how much ductwork it can support.

We tested a sampling of different-size collectors ranging from a 1-hp single-stage unit to 3½-hp cyclone. The testing protocol was similar to that used for our review of 1½-hp collectors. We used the results to estimate how much ductwork each machine might support while delivering the baseline performance of 800 cfm and 4,000 fpm.

Which equipment is right for you? This survey should help clarify your choices.

A Single-Stage Portable Works for Smaller Shops and Budgets

For a woodworker with a garage shop that includes a tablesaw, jointer, planer, and bandsaw, and with $600 or less to spend on dust collection, the most practical choice is a single-stage dust collector.

A 1-hp collector is the least expensive, but you'll be disappointed with its performance—about 450 cfm at best. Unless your larger machines have efficient dust-collection hoods or ports (extremely rare), that's not enough.

A Shop Vac Isn't Enough

hoices in dust collection range from light-duty shop vacs to powerful cyclone-style dust collectors. A shop vac might be your first dust collector, but it shouldn't be your last. Shop vacs can handle the dust from small tools, but are undermatched for the amount of waste that a stationary machine can throw. In choosing the collector, consider how frequently you use machines that produce large volumes of dust and chips. You also should weigh whether you need a collector that can support long segments of ductwork.

SINGLE-STAGE DUST COLLECTOR

The strongest of these, 2-hp and 3-hp units, can collect dust effectively from a tablesaw or other large woodworking machine through several feet of duct or hose. Units rated at 1½ hp can deliver top performance only through a short length of hose. The 1-hp units shouldn't be relied on to clear all the debris from large machines. Prices range from $150 for a 1-hp collector to $500 for a 3-hp unit.

TWO-STAGE CYCLONE

These units move more air with the same horsepower as their single-stage counterparts, offering as much capacity as most home shops are likely to need. If you want complete freedom on shop layout and ductwork, this is your best bet. Prices start around $750.

Single- or Two-Stage Dust Collector?

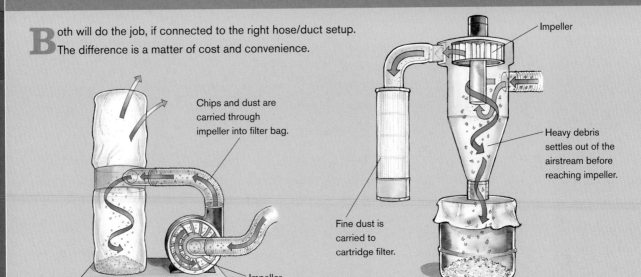

Both will do the job, if connected to the right hose/duct setup. The difference is a matter of cost and convenience.

Impeller

Chips and dust are carried through impeller into filter bag.

Impeller

Heavy debris settles out of the airstream before reaching impeller.

Fine dust is carried to cartridge filter.

SINGLE STAGE

A single-stage dust collector carries all of the debris past its impeller and then separates it into heavy chips and lightweight dust. It is the more affordable option.

TWO-STAGE CYCLONE

A two-stage cyclone allows larger debris to fall out of the airstream before it reaches the blower. This lets the fan spin more freely while being more efficiently shrouded, increasing airflow. The filter sees far less dust, and so doesn't need much maintenance.

WE TESTED THE CAPACITY OF EACH SYSTEM

Below is the amount of ductwork that each type of collector supported while maintaining 800 cfm and 4,000 linear fpm of airflow, enough to handle the chips and dust from any machine. We added flexible hose and a few typical connectors to simulate real-world conditions. Use these guidelines when choosing a collector and laying out your system.

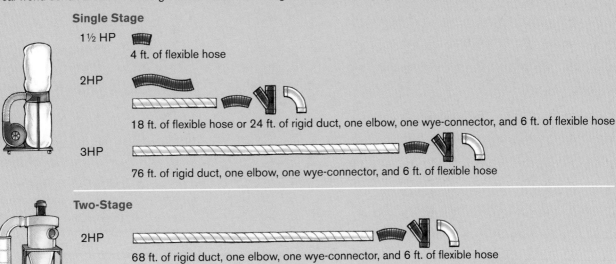

Single Stage

1½ HP

4 ft. of flexible hose

2HP

18 ft. of flexible hose or 24 ft. of rigid duct, one elbow, one wye-connector, and 6 ft. of flexible hose

3HP

76 ft. of rigid duct, one elbow, one wye-connector, and 6 ft. of flexible hose

Two-Stage

2HP

68 ft. of rigid duct, one elbow, one wye-connector, and 6 ft. of flexible hose

3½ HP

151 ft. of rigid duct, one elbow, one wye-connector, and 6 ft. of flexible hose

The 1½-hp collectors are the most powerful units that run on standard 110v current. They work well, given a minimum of flex hose and frequent cleaning of filters.

If you've got 220v power, though, consider stepping up one rung in class (and price). The 2-hp single-stage collector that we tested handled the equivalent of 18 ft. of flex hose before dropping below 800 cfm and 4,000 linear fpm.

Because the collector is mobile, you can wheel it from machine to machine, connecting it to each via a short length of hose. This ensures optimum performance at each machine, but sacrifices convenience.

An alternative is to park the collector in a central location and use wye connectors, blast gates, and a couple of hose runs to connect it to your most frequent offenders. This approach lets you operate a variety of woodworking machines without undoing and redoing dust-collector connections. Put machines that generate less dust at the farthest end of the hose. Use a shop vac to handle the lightest-duty machines.

It's worth pausing at this point to say a few words about filters. Dust smaller than 10 microns—about half the thickness of this page—can be inhaled far more easily than expelled; once lodged in the lungs, it can cause a host of health problems.

Many single-stage collectors come with woven fabric bags that, when new, capture particles as small as 30 microns. Their performance improves with use, as a layer of fine dust builds up on the filter surfaces. This works, but erratically: Plenty of hazardous dust escapes while the coating accumulates, and the coating will often release sudden puffs of ultrafine dust through the fabric and into the shop.

You will breathe easier with 1-micron filters, but they still require fairly frequent cleaning. In contrast, the accordion pleats of cartridge filters allow much more filter area in the same space, increasing intervals between cleanings by three to ten times.

A warning: Cartridge filters can be more delicate than cloth bags. A protective screen at the filter's intake is a good idea.

As a last word on single-stage collectors, there are more powerful units available. A 3-hp single-stage collector can be left in a corner and connected to a significant amount of pipe. The one we tested will provide sufficient airflow and velocity at the end of 76 ft. of ductwork, plus an elbow, a wye connector, and 6 ft. of hose. On the downside, the collector will take up about 10 sq. ft. of shop space, and you'll have four filter bags to clean, not just two. In addition, a collector in this 3-hp class costs about $500. Upgrading the filter bags, which often is necessary, might cost another $400. That's before ductwork.

Once you've reached that level of expense, it's worth considering a cyclone.

A Cyclone Is Best for Fixed Ductwork

The cyclones we tested range in price from $750 to $1,200 and come with good cartridge filtration. Any of them can quickly move high volumes of air through enough ductwork to span the length and width of a two-car garage. If you plan to spend $2,000 or so, the purchase price leaves plenty of cash for adding that duct-work. Your choice should be guided by your own shop layout.

The 2-hp unit we tested, for instance, can support roughly 68 ft. of ductwork, one 90-degree elbow, one wye connector, and 6 ft. of flex hose. The 3½-hp machine will handle larger loads. Tests show that it will deliver similar performance with up to 151 ft. of straight ductwork and the same elbow, wye connector, and length of flex hose. There are larger cyclones on the market, but they provide more capacity than a home shop is ever likely to need.

GARRETT HACK is a *Fine Woodworking* contributor, teacher, and professional furniture maker.

MICHAEL STANDISH provided research and testing for this article.

Two Ways to Use a Single-Stage Collector

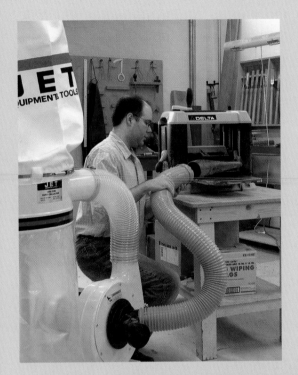

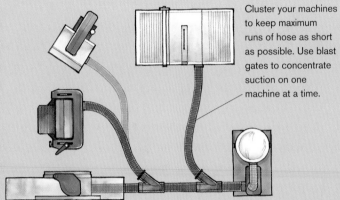

Cluster your machines to keep maximum runs of hose as short as possible. Use blast gates to concentrate suction on one machine at a time.

ONE MACHINE AT A TIME. Fitted with a short length of hose, a 1½-hp or 2-hp collector can be wheeled around the shop and connected to each machine as needed.

MULTIPLE MACHINES. More horsepower lets you park your collector. A 2-hp machine is strong enough to support about 18 ft. of flexible hose, which also allows for semipermanent connection to several machines at once.

Bigger Dust Collectors Offer More Shop Layout Options

THREE POSSIBLE DUCTWORK CONFIGURATIONS

Cyclone collectors are powerful enough to support permanent installations of fixed ductwork. Run ductwork along one wall (photo at right) and use branches of duct or flexible hose to reach machines. A diagonal duct run (left drawing below) mounted overhead, works well for tools in the middle of the room. A duct run around the shop's perimeter (right drawing below) can be mounted overhead or on the walls and works best for tools positioned along the walls.

ONE-WALL LAYOUT

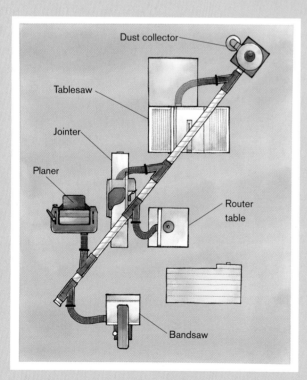

Diagonal layout

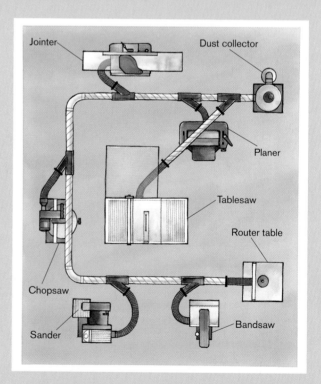

Perimeter layout

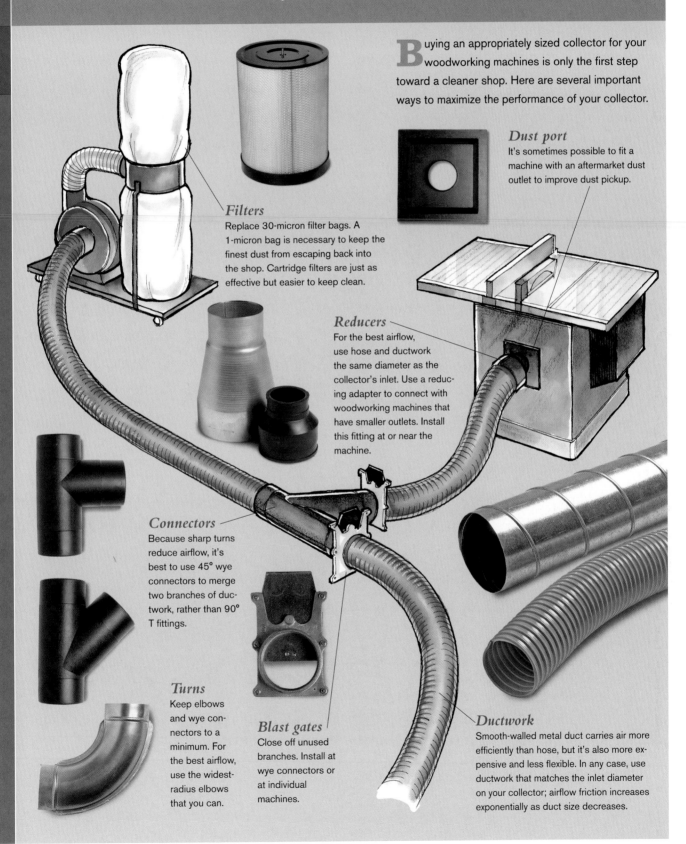

Buying an appropriately sized collector for your woodworking machines is only the first step toward a cleaner shop. Here are several important ways to maximize the performance of your collector.

Dust port
It's sometimes possible to fit a machine with an aftermarket dust outlet to improve dust pickup.

Filters
Replace 30-micron filter bags. A 1-micron bag is necessary to keep the finest dust from escaping back into the shop. Cartridge filters are just as effective but easier to keep clean.

Reducers
For the best airflow, use hose and ductwork the same diameter as the collector's inlet. Use a reducing adapter to connect with woodworking machines that have smaller outlets. Install this fitting at or near the machine.

Connectors
Because sharp turns reduce airflow, it's best to use 45° wye connectors to merge two branches of ductwork, rather than 90° T fittings.

Turns
Keep elbows and wye connectors to a minimum. For the best airflow, use the widest-radius elbows that you can.

Blast gates
Close off unused branches. Install at wye connectors or at individual machines.

Ductwork
Smooth-walled metal duct carries air more efficiently than hose, but it's also more expensive and less flexible. In any case, use ductwork that matches the inlet diameter on your collector; airflow friction increases exponentially as duct size decreases.

Plumbing a Shop for Air

BY ROLAND JOHNSON

I've used compressed air in my shop for more than 20 years. Originally, I bought a compressor for a spray gun and an air-powered sander, but over the years I've added brad and finish nailers, a vacuum-bag veneer press, vacuum clamps, drills, and routers. Compressed air, like electricity, is a wonderful source of power.

But many compressed-air systems are inadequate. A good one will supply an ample volume of air at a consistent pressure, free of moisture and particulate matter. With the right design, even a small compressed-air system can be effective, efficient, and clean. The diameter and length of the pipe that you use affect the pressure and volume of air it will deliver. You need larger diameters for longer runs to avoid drastic pressure drops in the system. Compressor manufacturers are a great planning resource and offer free charts and tables that you can use to size a system for your shop.

Iron Pipe Works Best

A number of different kinds of pipe will work well to distribute compressed air inside a shop. Copper pipe is relatively inexpensive, but its main drawback is that it requires a plumber's talent for sweating joints, and you need a torch to do that. In new construction this may be less of a hazard, but in older shops, sawdust settled into hidden crevices can be a real danger. I would never use rigid PVC because a sharp blow from the edge of a board could cause it to rupture and send shrapnel flying.

I chose black iron pipe (¾ in. dia. for the main header pipe and ½ in. dia. for the relatively short drops) because it's the most durable and offers the most flexibility for any future changes to my system. You can buy precut and threaded lengths of pipe and all the necessary fittings at most hardware and home stores. I borrowed a pipe threader and bought bulk lengths of pipe. That way I could cut the pipe to the exact lengths I needed, and I saved money to boot. Adding a few strategically placed threaded couplers or T-fittings to the system makes an iron-pipe system easy to modify or add on to as needs dictate.

The System Design Is Simple

A continuous-loop system, in which the pipe returns all the way back to the first drop line, is the best for keeping the pressure and volume consistent. But such a system would have required a lot more pipe than I had wanted to invest in, so I chose a system that dead ends, and it's been plenty adequate for my needs. Whichever design

Name That Fitting

When you shop for plumbing supplies, have in hand a sketch of the system you're building and a parts list of every length of pipe and fitting required. Knowing the right names for fittings ensures that you'll get what you need.

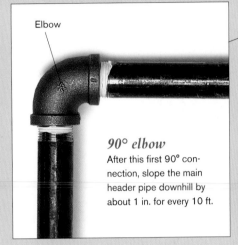

Elbow

90° elbow
After this first 90° connection, slope the main header pipe downhill by about 1 in. for every 10 ft.

Black T-fitting
Make the first leg a vertical run so that any moisture that condenses inside the pipe drains down and out of the system.

¾-in.-dia. main

T-fitting

THE AIR SUPPLY

Use a flexible hose to connect the compressor to the first pipe. The hose will prevent the noise and vibration of the compressor from spreading to the plumbing system, and the first vertical pipe will remove most of the moisture from the air.

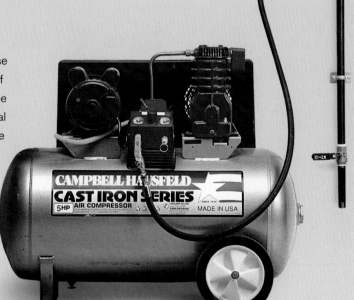

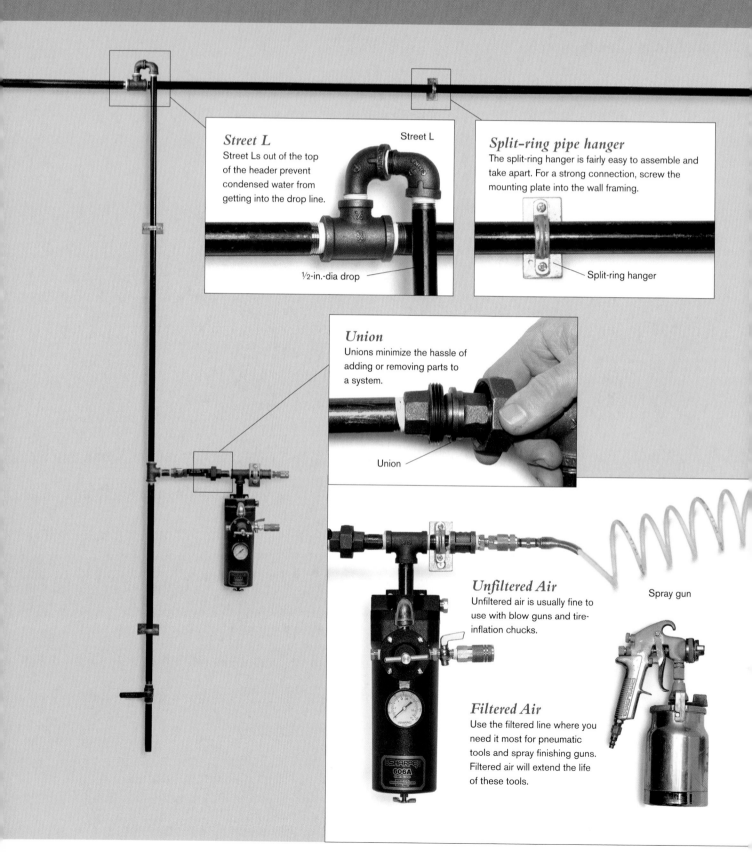

Street L
Street Ls out of the top of the header prevent condensed water from getting into the drop line.

Street L

½-in.-dia drop

Split-ring pipe hanger
The split-ring hanger is fairly easy to assemble and take apart. For a strong connection, screw the mounting plate into the wall framing.

Split-ring hanger

Union
Unions minimize the hassle of adding or removing parts to a system.

Union

Unfiltered Air
Unfiltered air is usually fine to use with blow guns and tire-inflation chucks.

Spray gun

Filtered Air
Use the filtered line where you need it most for pneumatic tools and spray finishing guns. Filtered air will extend the life of these tools.

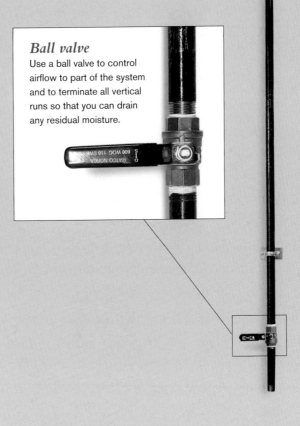

FILTERED AIR: YOU DON'T NEED IT FOR EVERYTHING

At least one drop line off the main header pipe ought to be equipped with a filter and regulator. I use a Sharpe (800-742-7731) model 606A air-control unit that has a reusable filter and a water drain. Expensive desiccant driers can extract remaining moisture and oil droplets from the compressed air, but unless you're setting up a regulation spray booth, the driers are overkill.

Ball valve
Use a ball valve to control airflow to part of the system and to terminate all vertical runs so that you can drain any residual moisture.

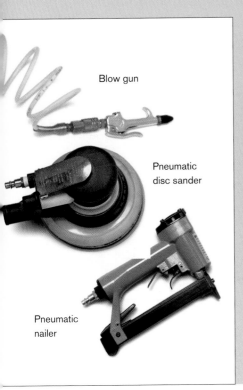

Blow gun

Pneumatic disc sander

Pneumatic nailer

you choose, you can control moisture and particulate matter fairly easily.

Water runs downhill, so you can get rid of most of it by sloping the main header pipe away from the compressor, using gravity to your advantage. Install ball valves at the end of each vertical drop line off the main header for drainage, and use a filter where needed to eliminate any remaining moisture and particulate matter. A good maintenance practice of opening the ball valves daily and regularly draining the compressor tank will go a long way toward keeping the system dry and clean.

Start with a ball valve attached to the compressor tank that can instantly shut off the airflow from the tank to the system, and use a flexible hose (rubber, metal-clad, or clear plastic) to connect the compressor to the first vertical length of pipe. The hose must be at least as large in diameter as the air outlet of the compressor. The flexible hose eliminates the transmission of vibrations that can cause undue noise and that could otherwise ultimately damage the piping system. Connect the flexible hose to the pipe with a T-fitting. From the T, one pipe extends up to meet the header that supplies air to all of the drops, and a second pipe extends down to another ball valve that is used to drain moisture from the system. Locate the main header pipe as close to the ceiling as possible.

Install T-fittings in the header wherever you need a drop line to bring the air down from the header to where it will be easy to access with a quick-connect hose coupler.

To minimize moisture getting into the drop lines, come out of the top of the T-fitting in the header by using two street Ls that create a 180-degree turn. Add another T-fitting in the drop to tap the air at a convenient height off the floor where you need it, and install a ball valve in that horizontal air supply so that you can shut off the air to that service without disrupting airflow to the rest of the system.

Add Filter/Regulators Where You Need Them

For most shops, a relatively inexpensive combination filter and regulator is all you need for clean, dry air. I use a unit that has a reusable filter and a water drain.

You also can add an oiler to a dedicated air drop line if you use that line to run only tools that need to be oiled regularly, but I would advise against it. For one thing, it would be easy to contaminate a hose or a spray gun accidentally if it were inadvertently hooked up to this line. Also, for most tools that need oil, it's enough to add a few drops directly into each tool as you use it.

ROLAND JOHNSON builds cabinets, restores old cars, and tinkers with his tractor on a farm in central Minnesota.

Wiring a Workshop

The electrical wiring, outlets, and lighting in your shop should be as specialized as your tools. It's hard to turn out high-quality work—or to work safely—in a poorly illuminated shop. It is equally frustrating and potentially dangerous if your tools keep tripping breakers on underpowered circuits or if your floor is a tangle of extension cords. To upgrade your workspace to meet the special needs of woodworking, you should know how to identify your needs and then communicate them to an electrician with the skills to turn your plan into reality. If you put these ideas to use, your woodworking will be safer and more satisfying.

Shop Features Dictate the Wiring Layout

Installing the wiring for a woodshop is done most easily during construction or remodeling with the walls open, but it can be done anytime. If the walls are closed in, either have the wiring run in surface-mounted conduit or hire an "old work" electrician who can run wires in existing walls and make a minimum of holes to be patched later.

To feed the shop circuits, the best approach is to install an electrical subpanel (breaker box) specifically for the shop. In a well-designed system a breaker will rarely trip, but if it does, it helps to have the panel nearby. There's a wide range of subpanels available, and your choice will depend on how much power and how many circuits you need.

At any given time, most one-person shops will be running one major stationary tool, a dust collector, an air filtration system, and lights. In this case, 60 amps at 240/120v likely will provide enough power. If there's heating or air conditioning running as well, a 100-amp subpanel probably will be adequate. I suggest a panel with room for 16 or 20 circuit breakers. These are starting points. Because each shop is different, you should calculate the number of circuits and power needs of your own.

There are two interdependent aspects to wiring a shop. One is circuit design—how the various things that use power (called "loads") are arranged and grouped, and how they are connected to their electricity source through wiring and circuit breakers. The other is the choice and location of light fixtures, receptacles, and switches.

BY CLIFFORD A. POPEJOY

A BOOST IN SAFETY AND CONVENIENCE

Think about how you work, then plan to have ample power exactly where
you need it. The right array of circuits, switches, and outlets makes the shop
more pleasant to work in, and a few key accessories complete the picture.

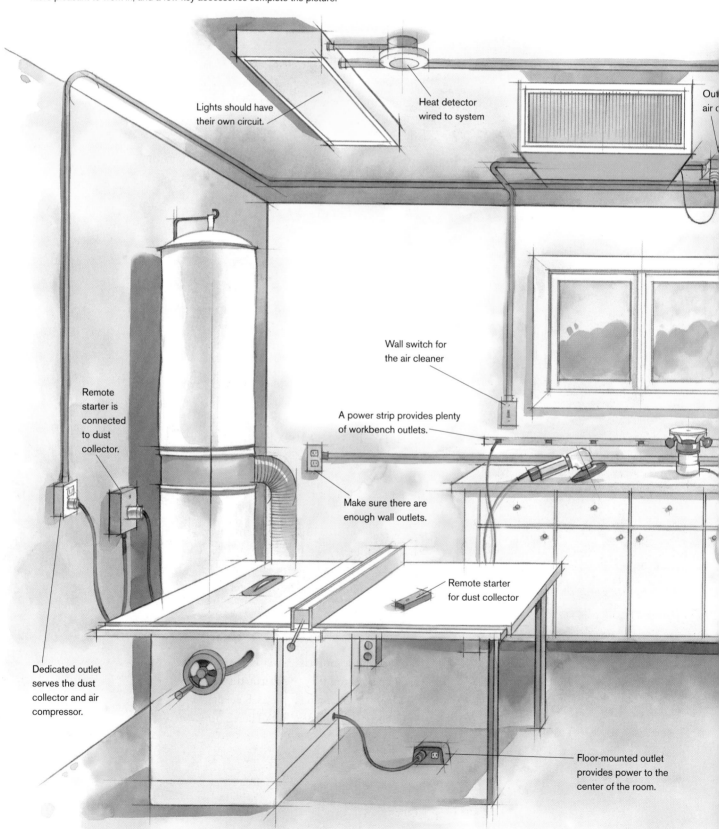

Lights should have
their own circuit.

Heat detector
wired to system

Out
air c

Wall switch for
the air cleaner

Remote
starter is
connected
to dust
collector.

A power strip provides plenty
of workbench outlets.

Make sure there are
enough wall outlets.

Remote starter
for dust collector

Dedicated outlet
serves the dust
collector and air
compressor.

Floor-mounted outlet
provides power to the
center of the room.

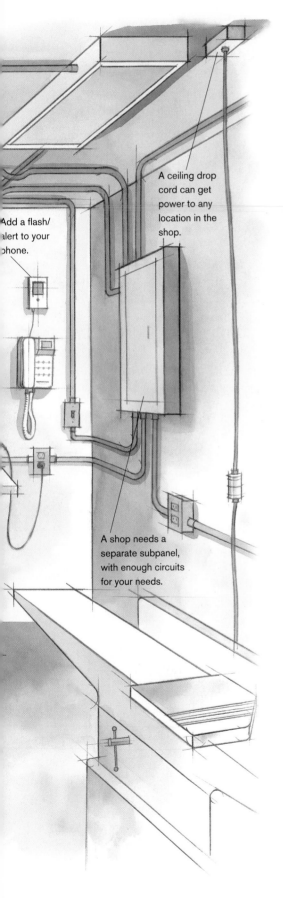

Add a flash/
alert to your
phone.

A ceiling drop
cord can get
power to any
location in the
shop.

A shop needs a
separate subpanel,
with enough circuits
for your needs.

Let There Be Light
(on its Own Circuit)

Depending on the size of the shop, you
should have one or more 120v, 15-amp circuits dedicated to lighting. That way if you
are ripping a board and your tablesaw trips
a breaker, you won't be plunged into dark-
ness and into a dangerous situation.

To compute how many lighting circuits
you will need, add up the total wattage of
the lights and provide one 15-amp lighting
circuit for every 1,500 watts. This is based
on loading each circuit to about 80 percent
of its capacity. This cushion, though not
required in noncommercial applications, is
still a good idea.

For example, to provide lighting for
a single-car garage-size shop (240 sq. ft.)
with 96-in., high-output (HO) fluorescent
lights, you would need four separate 2-lamp
fixtures. Each 8-ft. lamp requires 110 watts,
so you would need a total of 880 watts to
light this shop. Consider installing some
task lighting (say a track fixture with three
65-watt floodlamps or equivalent fluorescent floods) as well. I'd put this lighting
on one 15-amp circuit.

Consider setting up the lighting so that
the general lighting fixtures are wired to
two or more separate switches, with the
task lights switched separately from the
general lighting. This way, if your machine
and bench areas are separate, you can save
energy by illuminating only the area in
which you're working.

Outlets: The More the Better

It's a fact that a shop can never have too
many clamps, and it's equally true that it
can't have too many receptacles. Receptacles
should go on 20-amp circuits. There's no
limit set by the National Electrical Code
(NEC) for the number of outlets that can go
on a circuit in a residential application. For
a shop, it makes sense to identify the loads
you expect to operate at the same time and

Plan Circuit by Circuit

Designing the wiring for your shop is pretty simple if you approach it piece by piece. Start by determining your lighting needs, then provide power for receptacles serving portable power tools. Finally, work out the requirements for stationary machines that might run simultaneously.

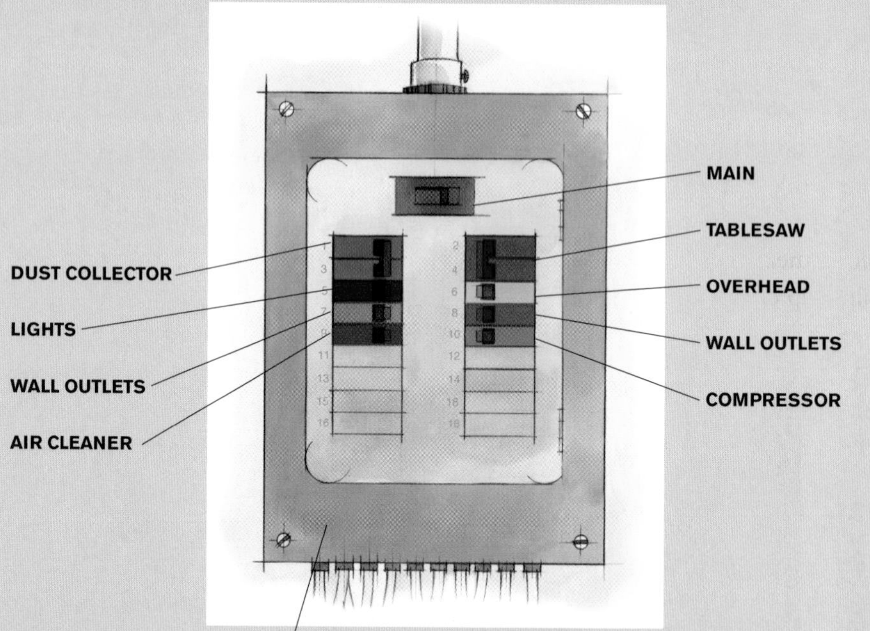

DUST COLLECTOR

LIGHTS

WALL OUTLETS

AIR CLEANER

MAIN

TABLESAW

OVERHEAD

WALL OUTLETS

COMPRESSOR

SYMBOL KEY

$ Switch

220v outlet

Standard outlet

Ceiling outlet

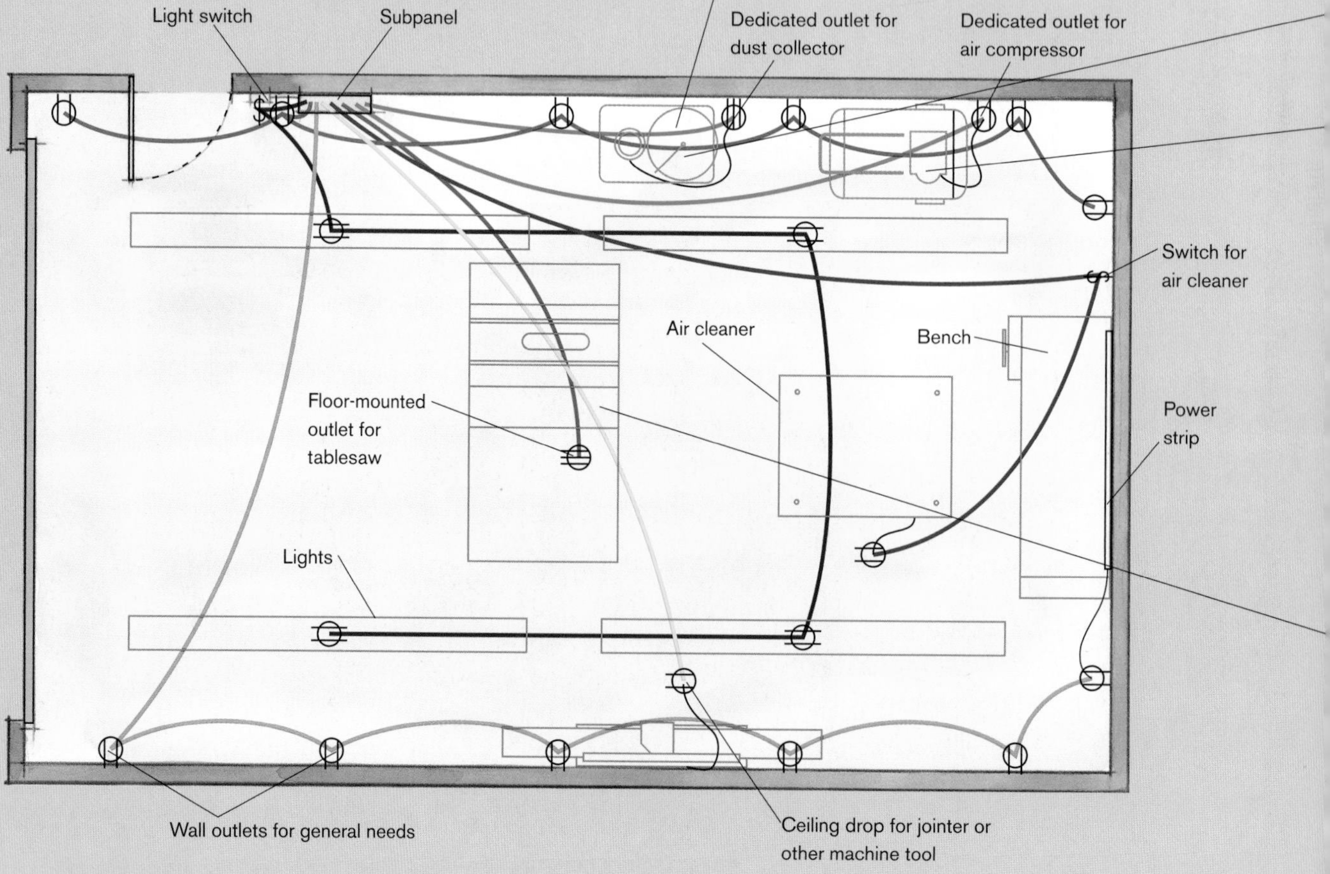

Light switch

Subpanel

Dedicated outlet for dust collector

Dedicated outlet for air compressor

Switch for air cleaner

Air cleaner

Bench

Floor-mounted outlet for tablesaw

Power strip

Lights

Wall outlets for general needs

Ceiling drop for jointer or other machine tool

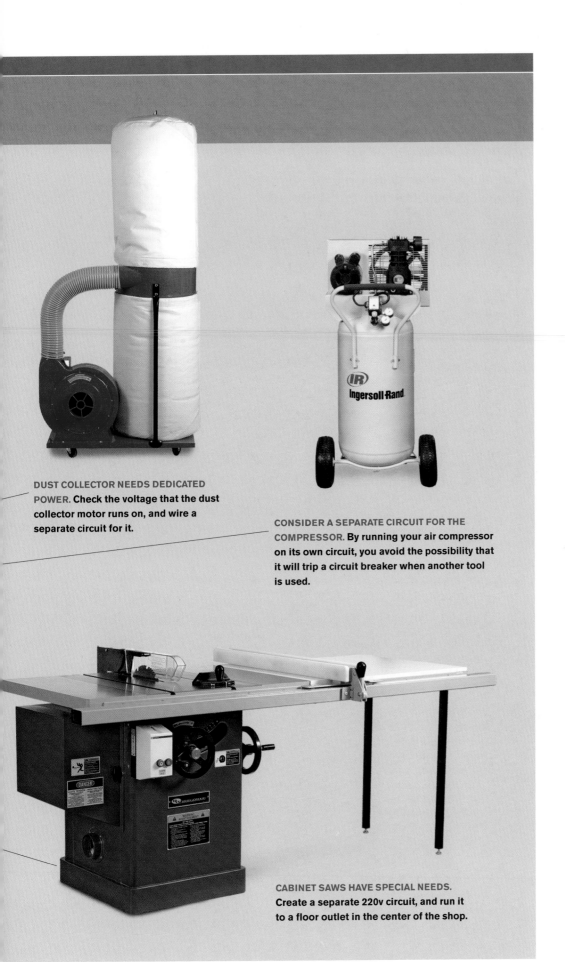

DUST COLLECTOR NEEDS DEDICATED POWER. Check the voltage that the dust collector motor runs on, and wire a separate circuit for it.

CONSIDER A SEPARATE CIRCUIT FOR THE COMPRESSOR. By running your air compressor on its own circuit, you avoid the possibility that it will trip a circuit breaker when another tool is used.

CABINET SAWS HAVE SPECIAL NEEDS. Create a separate 220v circuit, and run it to a floor outlet in the center of the shop.

Get the Power Where You Need It

CEILING One way to avoid having power cords strewn about your shop floor is to use a ceiling-mounted drop cord. This brings power to the middle of your shop in a convenient and safe way. Just roll out the tool of choice and plug away.

WORKBENCH POWER. A Plugmold power strip gives you a convenient place to plug in power tools that are used often at your workbench.

FLOOR Another way to bring power to the middle of your shop is to use a monument-style receptacle. This type avoids the problems of a flush-mounted receptacle, which include dust clogging and possible shorts from metal objects.

group the receptacles onto circuits so that each circuit can comfortably support the expected demand. A 120v, 20-amp circuit can provide 2,400 watts, although it's a good idea to keep the load to 80 percent or less, or about 1,900 watts. To figure out how many circuits are needed, look at the power needed as shown on the tool nameplate (some nameplates will specify watts, and some amps). If the tool specs give amps only, convert from amps to watts for a 120v tool by multiplying amps times 120. For instance, if you have a small air compressor that draws 13 amps (1,560 watts), put in a receptacle supplied by its own 20-amp circuit, called a "dedicated" circuit. For outlets that won't be supplying a specific tool, as in an area like an assembly bench where you will be using various small power tools, I suggest three or four outlets on a 20-amp circuit.

The NEC requires ground fault circuit interrupter (GFCI) protection for any 15-amp or 20-amp branch circuits supplying a garage or other work area at grade level. You can meet this requirement by using a GFCI circuit breaker or by having a GFCI receptacle first in line and wired to protect the downstream receptacles.

For general-use outlets, like the ones used for routers, hand-sanders, and corded drills, it is a good idea to set up circuits based on the area served. For example, you might set up a separate circuit for each wall. Or you may want a couple of 20-amp circuits to serve your workbench, where you might have three or four outlets on each circuit. A neat trick is to run two circuits along the wall and feed alternating receptacles from the two different circuits. Don't use a shared neutral circuit for this; you have to GFCI-protect the outlets, and keeping the two circuits completely separate makes this easier.

A product called Plugmold® (www. wiremold.com) is useful for providing workbench power. It is a steel channel with outlets spaced at intervals. Plugmold stands about 1¼ in. wide and above the surface and is available in various receptacle spacings (12 in. is best for shop use). Plugmold is much sturdier than a typical cord-connected "power strip" and is the right way to pack a lot of outlets along a wall.

It's a good idea to place wall outlets 50 in. above the floor (to the bottom of the box). That way if you lean sheet goods against the wall, they won't cover the outlets. And the outlets will be well above any benchtop or other work surface. Another nice setup is to set aside a shelf area for cordless-tool chargers and put a 3-plus-ft. strip of Plugmold with 6-in. receptacle spacing on the wall behind the shelf. Put this on a separate 20-amp circuit, so you can leave it powered up while turning the other receptacle circuits off at the breakers for safety when you're not in the shop.

Get Plenty of Juice to Stationary Tools

The big guns—stationary tablesaw, jointer, planer, dust collector—draw so much power that each requires its own circuit. (Without it, running two simultaneously will trip a breaker.) If the motor can be set up to run on 240v, have an electrician do it. It will probably require taking the motor out of the machine. There's no power efficiency advantage to running a machine at 240v vs. 120v in a single-phase system, but the higher voltage means lower amperage, and as a result, you can use smaller-gauge power-supply wiring. That translates into less expense to run the wire and to hook it up.

To figure out what size circuits you will need, check the amp rating on each tool's data plate or in its product manual. Keep in mind that the circuit breaker at the subpanel is designed to protect the building's wiring from an overcurrent condition—it does not, however, ensure that the machine's motor won't overload.

If the motor does not have an internal circuit breaker for overload protection (the tool manual will indicate this), a fused disconnect may be required. Ask the electrician to install it. The fuses in the disconnect box will protect the motor windings from overheating.

Some tools are an island—getting power to a machine in the middle of the floor can be a challenge. You don't want a cord running along the floor that you might trip over. If there's a basement or crawlspace below, I would run cable or conduit below the floor and use a monument-style housing to hold the receptacle at the base of the machine (see the bottom photo on p. 206). A flush-mounted floor outlet is a poor choice for a shop. It will fill with debris and could be shorted out by a stray nail or staple.

If you plan to move shop machines around and you want to keep the floor clear, use a hanging (pendant) outlet about 6 ft. to 7 ft. above the floor. To prevent accidental unplugging, a locking cord cap on the receptacle end of the pendant outlet is a good idea (see the left photo on p. 206). This will require you to put a compatible locking plug on the machine cord, or make an adapter.

Custom Touches Add Safety, Convenience

Even though they are full of flammable materials, most woodshops have no smoke alarms. That is because airborne sawdust can set off the photo-ionization or photo-electric sensors typically used in smoke alarms to detect smoke. The solution is to install a heat-detecting fire alarm that can activate the smoke alarms in the house. Firex® (www.icca.invensys.com/firex) has a complete line of smoke alarms that includes compatible heat-detector units.

It's nice to have a phone in the shop, but how do you hear it ring while planing boards and wearing hearing protectors? You can add a flashing visual alert.

Another convenience is to have your dust collector start automatically when you switch on a machine it serves. It's possible to build a current sensor/relay setup, but there are commercially available ones. Ecogate® (www.ecogate.com) sells a system that not only turns on the dust collector when it senses that a tool has started, but also opens and closes the adjacent blast gate. Alternatively, you could install a relay and receiver on the dust collector's cord that switches on and off with a remote-control transmitter that can sit in a convenient spot or hang on your key ring (like a car-door remote).

Work with Your Electrician

Unless you're a qualified electrician or are willing to take the time to become familiar with the techniques of the trade, the many requirements of the NEC, and any local codes pertinent to shop wiring, you should find a licensed electrician or electrical contractor to wire your shop. Look for one who does both residential and commercial work; a strictly residential electrician might not be familiar with some of the products and design elements suggested here.

When working with an electrician, it's more productive to explain the objective or goal than to try to dictate a precise method or approach. Sit down with the electrician before work begins, and lay out your requirements clearly. If your plan and goals are not clear at the outset, be prepared to pay for changes.

Finally, don't expect to find an electrician who will "just do the hookups" after you've pulled the wires, etc. Few licensed electricians will take the risk of putting the finishing touches on work they didn't do themselves.

CLIFFORD A. POPEJOY is a licensed electrical contractor and occasional woodworker in Sacramento, California.

Consider These Useful Accessories

TELEPHONE FLASHER If your shop has a telephone, it will be impossible to hear when you are wearing earplugs and operating loud machinery. This device uses a flashing light to let you know that you have a call.

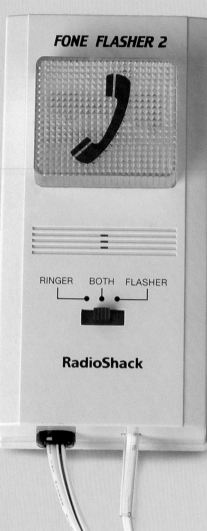

HEAT DETECTOR Airborne wood dust can cause false alarms with a standard smoke detector. A heat detector can warn you of a shop fire and can be wired into your home fire-detection system if the shop is in a detached building.

REMOTE-CONTROL TRANSMITTER SWITCH A remote-control receiver is connected between the dust collector's power cord and the receptacle. A small transmitter lets you turn the collector on and off from anywhere in the shop. This will save you a few steps and let you devote more attention to your work.

Fire Safety
in the Shop

BY BRUCE RYDEN

No matter the size of your shop, fire hazards are present day in and day out. Wood is a combustible material, but when it's in the form of a solid mass, such as a plank of lumber, it is difficult to ignite and to keep burning. Try holding a match to a large piece of wood and see which gets burned first, the wood or your fingers. If you took that same piece of wood, put it through a thickness planer, and held a match to the pile of shavings, you'd be amazed by how quickly it would ignite.

The best way to prevent a fire in your shop is to practice good housekeeping. Sawdust and wood shavings are the two most common dangerous products in a woodshop. They are ignited easily, and the fire can spread with unbelievable speed and intensity. The careless use, storage, and disposal of finishing supplies also are frequently encountered fire hazards. Many woodworkers store cans of varnish, containers of solvents and thinners, and organic-based finishes, such as linseed oil and tung oil, on open shelves in the shop, where they can provide the fuel to greatly accelerate the spread of a fire.

Prevention Is Mostly Common Sense

Three elements are required to cause a fire: fuel, oxygen, and a source of heat. Take away any one of them, and you cannot have combustion.

We need the oxygen to breathe, so we can't remove that. We often can remove the heat to prevent a fire (by not smoking or not using torches or welding equipment in a woodshop). But the easiest item to remove is the fuel. It may seem like a real chore to sweep up a pile of wood chips or shavings after a long day working in the shop, but by cleaning up, you can remove the most manageable portion of the three elements needed to start a fire.

Electricity, another hazard in most shops, often is blamed as the cause of a fire, but seldom is that borne out by a competent fire investigation. In a clean shop, this heat source rarely is the cause of a fire. If an electrical short circuit does occur, it must have a fuel to feed upon. Without contact with piles of sawdust or wood shavings, the likelihood of a short circuit starting a shop fire is improbable (but possible). Still, any tool or piece of machinery that has a cord that is frayed, cracked, or otherwise not in great condition

IT COULD HAVE BEEN WORSE. Ellis Walentine, host of Webcentral.com, lost his entire shop in rural Pennsylvania in May 1999 to a fire, but no one was hurt in the conflagration. He suspects the fire was caused when arcing in a loose connection in the electrical panel ignited some accumulated sawdust.

Preventing a Fire in the Shop

DISPOSE OF OILY RAGS.
Rags soaked with flammable finishes can ignite spontaneously, so they must be disposed of properly. With its spring-loaded, self-closing lid, this red bucket prevents spontaneous combustion. A plastic bucket half-filled with water also will work.

STORE FLAMMABLE LIQUIDS. A storage cabinet for flammable liquids is meant to keep a fire from getting much worse very quickly. Whether you buy one or build your own (see below), it should have a self-closing door and a lip on the shelves to keep spilled liquids from escaping. The metal cabinet above costs about $850.

A SHOP-BUILT SOLUTION TO STORING FLAMMABLE LIQUIDS

Ryden built a basic storage cabinet for flammables in the garage adjacent to his shop. He used 2x4s for the frame, and covered that with two layers of drywall. He encased the edges of the drywall with aluminum channel to keep the gypsum from crumbling. By hinging the door at the top, it self-closes when he removes the strut that holds the door open so he can access the shelf inside.

CONSTRUCTION DETAIL

The 2x4 frame serves as a spillproof lip on the front of the shelf. The two layers of drywall greatly increase the time that it would take a fire to ignite the liquids in the cabinet.

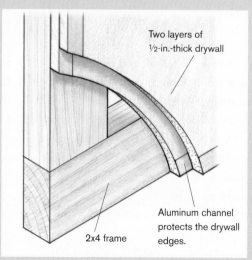

Two layers of
½-in.-thick drywall

Aluminum channel
protects the drywall
edges.

2x4 frame

should be replaced, and all electrical connections should be secured tightly.

One of the frequently forgotten and least understood causes of fire in the shop is spontaneous combustion of rags and waste. When an organic oil, such as linseed oil or tung oil, is applied to rags used for finishing, a heating process takes place. This heating takes place only in the presence of oxygen, and when the heat given off by the process is not allowed to dissipate, it will continue until the rags reach a temperature that is high enough to ignite them.

By placing used rags in a steel container with water and a cover on it, this process will not occur. An acceptable alternative is to hang the rags in a single layer on a clothesline or a fence, which allows the rags to dry without the heat buildup.

The application of a flammable finish by hand is not without hazards, but if there is good air exchange with fresh outside air, the vapors given off by the finish can be diluted to a safe level. Most of these vapors are heavier than air and will sink to the floor. Be especially careful about any possible source of ignition (such as water heaters, furnaces, portable heaters, and electric fans) down near the floor close to where you are working.

The proper storage of flammable and combustible materials used in finishing projects is one of the most neglected safety issues in many workshops. Cans and sometimes even glass bottles stored on open shelves can fall off and release large quantities of hazardous materials. Spray cans containing any flammable or combustible materials are extremely dangerous items to have sitting on open shelves. These cans are considered by the National Fire Protection Association as the most hazardous of all flammable or combustible materials. Once ignited, finish supplies quickly can turn a small fire into a dangerous, raging inferno.

Commercially available storage cabinets for finishes can be expensive. But for small home shops, you can make your own inexpensive version by surrounding the contents on all sides with two layers of ½-in.-thick drywall, which will greatly slow the speed with which a fire will spread to the finishes inside the cabinet (see the facing page). The door should be self-closing, and the shelves should be lipped to contain any spilled liquid.

Equip the Shop with Heat Detectors

The most sensitive detection device is the human nose, which can smell smoke long before any electronic gadget can detect it. But when you're not in the shop, you must rely on other detection devices. Electronic detectors fall into three major categories: heat, smoke, and flames. Of these, heat detectors are best for a woodworking shop. Smoke-detection devices—both the ionization type and the photoelectric type—are susceptible to false alarms caused by the dust generated in a woodshop. Flame detectors are not as susceptible to dust contamination, but they are much more expensive than heat detectors.

There are three types of heat detectors: fixed temperature, rate of rise, and a combination of both types. The fixed-temperature devices usually are set in the 135°F to 165°F range. When the temperature of the room reaches the preset level, the alarm sounds. The rate-of-rise detectors measure how quickly the room temperature increases. When it rises more than a certain number of degrees in a preset time period, the alarm sounds. The combination-type detector is the best for woodworking shops because it will sound the alarm as soon as it detects either a slow, smoldering fire or a quickly spreading fire. This alarm can be either a local alarm (sounding just inside or outside of the shop), or you can connect it to a monitored service (such as ADT or Brinks).

Three elements are required to cause a fire: fuel, oxygen, and a source of heat. Take away any one of them, and you cannot have combustion.

Combating a Fire in the Shop

If a fire occurs, damage will be minimized if a sprinkler system has been installed (top left). Heat detectors (right) provide an early warning and don't commonly suffer malfunctions in dusty environments. A fire extinguisher (bottom right) can prevent a small fire from getting worse, but you should always call the fire department first.

HEAT DETECTOR. Smoke detectors can malfunction because of the dust found in the air of most wood-shops. Heat detectors are a better choice in dusty environments. They are activated when the room temperature reaches a preset level, usually 135°F to 165°F. The heat detector in Ryden's shop is powered by a circuit from the electrical service panel, and it is connected to a commercial alarm service through a telephone line.

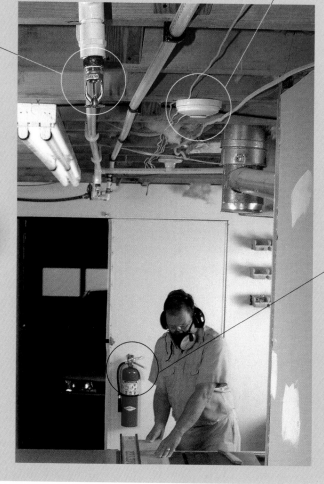

AUTOMATIC SPRINKLER SYSTEM. A typical sprinkler head will spray an area about 10 ft. by 10 ft. You can connect sprinklers to copper, galvanized, or PVC plastic pipes. PVC is the least expensive to install. Prime the pieces first with a cleaner, then daub on the cement.

FIRE EXTINGUISHER. Use an extinguisher rated ABC to fight woodshop fires fueled by wood, finishing supplies, or bad electrical connections. Extinguishers should always be placed near an exit so you won't get trapped by a fire while trying to access the extinguisher.

Putting Out a Fire Once it Starts

Although detection devices are good to have in the shop, they do nothing to slow or stop the spread of a fire. This is best done by an automatic sprinkler system that utilizes water to be discharged only in the vicinity of the fire, most often extinguishing the fire before it can spread. Most of us would rather come into the shop and find some water damage than find that the entire shop has been destroyed. There are systems that can be installed to detect water flowing through the sprinkler piping and sound an alarm, thereby reducing the water damage.

Sprinkler heads are readily available and inexpensive. (I paid a sprinkler contractor about $5 each for the ones I installed in my shop.) The total cost to plumb my 900-sq.-ft. shop with sprinklers was less than $100, and it took me eight hours to accomplish—a small price for a lot of peace of mind.

The most common sprinkler heads are the pendant style, which hang below the piping, and the upright style, which stand above the piping. They must be installed in the correct position or they will not function properly. In most shop situations the pendant head is appropriate. These heads are available from local fire-sprinkler contractors, but you also can find some online suppliers by doing a Web search for "fire sprinklers." The only application where water-sprinkler heads are not appropriate is in an unheated shop in a cold climate.

Place Extinguishers Near an Exit

Every shop should have at least one well-maintained, easily accessible, portable fire extinguisher. Fire extinguishers are first-aid appliances. You must know when to use them and when to back off and let a professional handle the situation. The first thing you should do when a fire is detected is to call the fire department. They can always go home if they're not needed.

Fires are classified into four different categories: A, B, C, and D. The easiest way I know to remember them is as follows: Category A involves anything that leaves ash when it burns (paper, wood, cloth); B involves burning liquid (gasoline, paint, paint thinners, oil-based products); C includes circuit fires (live electrical fires in wiring, wiring devices, motors, electrical appliances); and category D fires involve combustible metals, which usually are not found in woodworking shops.

The most effective fire extinguisher for a shop is at least a 10-lb. multipurpose dry-chemical fire extinguisher, rated ABC on the label. This type of extinguisher can be applied to any kind of fire in a shop, has sufficient agent to extinguish almost any fire in its early stage, and can be used with minimal training.

Another consideration with fire extinguishers is where to place them. You should always have to go toward an exit door to access the extinguisher. That way, if the fire suddenly builds, you have a way out of the shop without having to go past the fire. Always keep a door at your back when using a fire extinguisher. Never allow a fire to come between you and a safe way out.

BRUCE RYDEN is a retired fire-safety inspector.

Sources of Supply

Sprinklers
Sprinkler heads can be purchased from either a sprinkler-installation contractor or a plumbing-supply store.

Heat detectors
Heat detectors are offered at most electrical-supply stores and at many online suppliers.

Fire extinguishers
Fire extinguishers are available at most hardware stores and home centers.

Credits

The articles in this book appeared in the following issues of *Fine Woodworking.* All photos and drawings are courtesy *Fine Woodworking.*

pp. i–3 All photos © The Taunton Press, Inc.

p. 4: A Shop on Top by Paul H. Breskin, issue 174. Photos by Tom Begnal, © The Taunton Press, Inc.; Drawings by Brian Jensen, © The Taunton Press, Inc.

p. 8: The Shop as a Tool by Joe Tracy, issue 129. Photos by Vincent Laurence, © The Taunton Press, Inc.; Drawings by Design Core, © The Taunton Press, Inc.

p. 13: Great Shop in a Two-Car Garage by Curtis Erpelding, issue 131. Photos by Curtis Erpelding, © The Taunton Press, Inc.; Drawings by Design Core, © The Taunton Press, Inc.

p. 21: Turning a Parking Space into a Great Shop by Chris Gochnour, issue 141. Photos by Jonathan Binzen, © The Taunton Press, Inc.; Drawings by Design Core, © The Taunton Press, Inc.

p. 29: Smart Shop in a One-Car Garage by Matthew Teague, issue 160. Photos by Michael Pekovich, © The Taunton Press, Inc.; Drawings by Brian Jensen, © The Taunton Press, Inc.

p. 40: A Well-Organized One-Man Shop by Ross Day, issue 153. Photos by Terry Reed, © The Taunton Press, Inc., except p. 40 by Anatole Burkin, © The Taunton Press, Inc.; Drawings by Toby Wells @ Design Core, © The Taunton Press, Inc.

p. 47: A Layout Kit for Small Shops by John Yurko, issue 174. Photos by Asa Christana, © The Taunton Press, Inc.; Drawings by John Yurko, © The Taunton Press, Inc.

p. 52: A Shop Built Around an Island by Alan DeVilbiss, issue 181. Photos by Mark Schofield, © The Taunton Press, Inc.; Drawings by John Hartman, © The Taunton Press, Inc.

p. 57: A Shop in the Backyard by Rick Mc-Caskill, issue 167. Photos on pp. 57 and 61

by Dean Della Ventura, © The Taunton Press, Inc.; Photos on pp. 59 and 60 by Tom Begnal, © The Taunton Press, Inc.; Drawings by Vince Babak, © The Taunton Press, Inc.

p. 62: A Shop Inspired by School Memories by Mark Bellonby, issue 167. Photos by Rodney Diaz, © The Taunton Press, Inc.; Drawings by Toby Wells @ Design Core, © The Taunton Press, Inc.

p. 68: From the Ground Up by William Duck-worth, issue 181. Photos by Jonathan Binzen, © The Taunton Press, Inc.; Drawings by Vince Babak, © The Taunton Press, Inc.

p. 72: Dream Shop in the Woods by Les Cizek, issue 160. Photos by Tim Sams, © The Taunton Press, Inc.; Drawings by Vince Babak, © The Taunton Press, Inc.

p. 80: A Timber-Frame Dream by Eric Foertsch, issue 188. Photos by David Heim, © The Taunton Press, Inc.; Drawings by Vince Babak, © The Taunton Press, Inc.

p. 84: A Workshop Steeped in History by Eugene Landon, issue 174. Photos by Mark Schofield, © The Taunton Press, Inc.

p. 90: Quick-to-Make Tool Cabinet by Jan Zoltowski, issue 188. Photos by Mark Scho-field, © The Taunton Press, Inc.; Drawings by Bob La Pointe, © The Taunton Press, Inc.

p. 99: Basement Shop on Wheels by Anatole Burkin, issue 153. Photos by Michael Pekovich, © The Taunton Press, Inc.

p. 106: Not Your Father's Pegboard by Hank Gilpin, issue 130. Photos by Jonathan Binzen, © The Taunton Press, Inc.

p. 108: Three Ways to Rack Lumber by Matthew Teague, issue 130. Photo on p. 108 by Timothy Schreiner, © The Taunton Press, Inc.; Photo on p. 109 by Jonathan Binzen, © The Taunton Press, Inc.; Photo (left) on p. 110 by Strother Purdy, © The Taunton Press, Inc.; Photo (right) on p. 110 by Joe Romero, © The Taunton Press, Inc.; Drawings by Jim Richey, © The Taunton Press, Inc.

p. 111: Lumber Storage Solutions by Andy Beasley, issue 177. Photos by Tom Begnal, © The Taunton Press, Inc.; Drawings by Jim Richey, © The Taunton Press, Inc.

p. 116: Fine-Tune Your Shop by Jerry H. Lyons, issue 170. Photos by Mark Schofield, © The Taunton Press, Inc.; Drawings by Jim Richey, © The Taunton Press, Inc.

p. 121: Roll-Away Workshop by Bill Endress, issue 167. Photos by Matt Berger, © The Taunton Press, Inc.; Drawings by Brian Jensen, © The Taunton Press, Inc.

p. 128: Four Ways to Get Organized by Dave Padgett, issue 160. Photos by Anatole Burkin, © The Taunton Press, Inc.; except pp. 128 (bottom left) and 135 by Leroy Trujillo, © The Taunton Press, Inc.; Drawings by Melanie J. Powell, © The Taunton Press, Inc.

p. 136: Clamp Storage Solutions by John West, issue 164. Photo on p. 136 by William Duckworth, © The Taunton Press, Inc.; Photo on p. 139 by Barbara Duerr, © The Taunton Press, Inc.; Photo on p. 141 by Dean Della Ventura, © The Taunton Press, Inc.; Drawings by Jim Richey, © The Taunton Press, Inc.

p. 144: Low-Cost Shop Floor by Scott Gibson, issue 160. Photos by Tim Sams, © The Taunton Press, Inc.; Drawings by Vince Babak, © The Taunton Press, Inc.

p. 149: Shop Flooring Solutions by Anatole Burkin, issue 174. Photos by Marcia Ryan, © The Taunton Press, Inc.; except on pp. 147, 150 (left), 151 (top), 152 (far left), and 154 by Matthew Gardner, © The Taunton Press, Inc.

p. 156: Heating Your Shop by Andy Engel, issue 181. Photo on p. 156 by Michael Pekovich, © The Taunton Press, Inc.; Photos on p. 162 courtesy Louisville Tin and Stove, Empire Comfort Systems, Toyotomi; Photos on p. 163 courtesy Empire Comfort Systems, Vermont Castings, Schwank Heaters, Friedrich; Drawings by Brian Jensen, © The Taunton Press, Inc.

p. 164: Lighting for the Workshop by Jack L. Lindsey, issue 154. Photos by Erica Marks, © The Taunton Press, Inc.; except pp. 165,

171, and 172 by William Duckworth, © The Taunton Press, Inc.; Drawings by Laura Lind, © The Taunton Press, Inc.

p. 173: Small-Shop Dust Collectors by Sandor Nagyszalanczy, issue 117. Photos by William Duckworth, © The Taunton Press, Inc.; except p. 178 by Sandor Nagyszalanczy, © The Taunton Press, Inc.; Drawings by Christopher Clapp, © The Taunton Press, Inc.

p. 179: Dust Collection for the One-Man Shop by Anatole Burkin, issue 141. Photos by Anatole Burkin, © The Taunton Press, Inc.; except on p. 179 by William Duckworth, © The Taunton Press, Inc.; Drawing by Vince Babak, © The Taunton Press, Inc.

p. 188: Dust Collection Demystified by Garrett Hack, issue 188. Photos by Steve Scott, © The Taunton Press, Inc.; Drawings by Stephen Hutchings, © The Taunton Press, Inc.

p. 196: Plumbing a Shop for Air by Roland Johnson, issue 160. Photos p. 197 by Kathleen Williams, © The Taunton Press, Inc.; Photos p. 199 by Erica Marks, © The Taunton Press, Inc.

p. 201: Wiring a Workshop by Clifford A. Popejoy, issue 188. Photos by Kelly J. Dunton, © The Taunton Press, Inc.; except p. 205 top left by Rodney Diaz, © The Taunton Press, Inc.; top right by Mark Schofield, © The Taunton Press, Inc.; bottom by Tom Begnal, © The Taunton Press, Inc.; Drawings by Brian Jensen, © The Taunton Press, Inc.

p. 210: Fire Safety in the Shop by Bruce Ryden, issue 174. Photos by William Duckworth, © The Taunton Press, Inc.; except p. 211 by Ellis Wallentine, © The Taunton Press, Inc. and p. 212 top left and top right by Rodney Diaz, © The Taunton Press, Inc.; Drawing by Vince Babak, © The Taunton Press, Inc.

The New Best of Fine Woodworking Series

A collection of the best articles from the last ten years of Fine Woodworking

WITHDRAWN

OTHER BOOKS IN THE SERIES

Designing Furniture

The Best of Fine Woodworking
From the editors of FWW
ISBN 1-56158-684-6
Product #070767
$17.95 U.S.
$25.95 Canada

Small Woodworking Shops

The Best of Fine Woodworking
From the editors of FWW
ISBN 1-56158-686-2
Product #070768
$17.95 U.S.
$25.95 Canada

Working with Routers

The Best of Fine Woodworking
From the editors of FWW
ISBN 1-56158-685-4
Product #070769
$17.95 U.S.
$25.95 Canada

Building Small Projects

The Best of Fine Woodworking
From the editors of FWW
ISBN 1-56158-730-3
Product #070791
$17.95 U.S.
$25.95 Canada

Designing and Building Cabinets

The Best of Fine Woodworking
From the editors of FWW
ISBN 1-56158-732-X
Product #070792
$17.95 U.S.
$25.95 Canada

Traditional Finishing Techniques

The Best of Fine Woodworking
From the editors of FWW
ISBN 1-56158-733-8
Product #070793
$17.95 U.S.
$25.95 Canada

Working with Handplanes

The Best of Fine Woodworking
From the editors of FWW
ISBN 1-56158-748-6
Product #070810
$17.95 U.S.
$25.95 Canada

Working with Tablesaws

The Best of Fine Woodworking
From the editors of FWW
ISBN 1-56158-749-4
Product #070811
$17.95 U.S.
$25.95 Canada

Workshop Machines

The Best of Fine Woodworking
From the editors of FWW
ISBN 1-56158-765-6
Product #070826
$17.95 U.S.
$25.95 Canada

Workstations and Tool Storage

The Best of Fine Woodworking
From the editors of FWW
ISBN 1-56158-785-0
Product #070838
$17.95 U.S.
$25.95 Canada

Traditional Projects

The Best of Fine Woodworking
From the editors of FWW
ISBN 1-56158-784-2
Product #070839
$17.95 U.S.
$25.95 Canada

Hand Tools

The Best of Fine Woodworking
From the editors of FWW
ISBN 1-56158-783-4
Product #070840
$17.95 U.S.
$25.95 Canada

Spray Finishing

The Best of Fine Woodworking
From the editors of FWW
ISBN 1-56158-829-6
Product #070875
$17.95 U.S.

lependence
Township
Library

rkston, Michigan

Independe
Townsh
Library

Clarkston, Mic

ce

Independence
Township
Library

Clarkston, Michigan

The New Best of Fine Woodworking Slipcase Set Volume 1

Designing Furniture
Working with Routers
Small Woodworking Shops
Designing and Building Cabinets
Building Small Projects
Traditional Finishing Techniques

From the editors of FWW
ISBN 1-56158-736-2
Product #070808
$85.00 U.S./$120.00 Canada

The New Best of Fine Woodworking Slipcase Set Volume 2

Working with Handplanes
Workshop Machines
Working with Tablesaws
Selecting and Using Hand Tools
Traditional Projects
Workstations and Tool Storage

From the editors of FWW
ISBN 1-56158-747-8
Product #070809
$85.00 U.S./$120.00 Canada